Living the Incarnation

For my Community

Living the Incarnation

Praying with Francis and Clare of Assisi

SISTER FRANCES TERESA osc

Foreword by Bishop Vincent Nichols

Franciscan Press

First published in the USA in 1996 by
Franciscan Press
Quincy University
1800 College Avenue
Quincy, IL 62301–2699

First published in Great Britain in 1993 by
Darton, Longman and Todd Ltd, London

ISBN 0–8199–0971–8

Library of Congress Cataloging-in-Publication Data

Frances Teresa, Sister.
    Living the incarnation: praying with Francis and Clare
of Assisi
/ Sister Frances Teresa; foreword by Vincent Nichols.
        p.   cm.
    Originally published: London: Darton, Longman, and
Todd, c1993.
    Includes bibliographical references.
    ISBN 0–8199–0971–8 (alk. paper)
    1. Francis, of Assisi, Saint, 1182–1226—Meditations.
    2. Clare, of Assisi, Saint, 1194–1253—Meditations.
    3. Prayer.   I. Title.
BX4700.F6F68   1996
271'.3022—dc20   96–14460
                                                         CIP

Scripture quotations in this publication are from
The Jerusalem Bible published and copyright 1966,
1967 and 1968 by Darton, Longman and Todd Ltd and
Doubleday and Co. Inc.

Cover: design by Leigh Hurlock

Phototypeset by Intype London Ltd
Printed and bound in Great Britain
by Redwood Books Ltd, Trowbridge, Wiltshire

Contents

Contents

Foreword

It is often said that one of the curses of modern living is that everything must be done at breakneck speed. While there is much truth in this, perhaps our bigger problem lies in coping with the complexities of everything we touch and attempt. Yet neither speed nor complexity are special to our age.

Think, for a moment, of St Francis of Assisi. He was engaged in active Christian ministry for less than twenty years. Yet his impact on the whole Christian family, and way beyond it, can hardly be overestimated. In his lifetime he moved with remarkable speed. But he did so by cutting away the complexities of life, seizing or being seized by its essential but demanding simplicity, and never being lost to that grip.

It is not the romantic attractiveness of St Francis which appeals so universally. Rather, I believe, it is the realisation, instinctive at least, that St Francis faced squarely all the key issues in human experience. He sought meaning and fulfilment first of all in wealth, social status, civic achievement and the heroism of battle. He found them wanting. He also explored the path of energetic good works, rebuilding dilapidated churches and establishing a new institutional arm in the Church. But even this was not sufficient. The core of his story, and of his appeal, is much simpler. It is that above all else he stood before God. He came out from every human hiding place, from behind every fig leaf, and put himself totally and fearlessly in the hands of the living God. And because he received wholeness and communion in that meeting, then he displayed his unique and irresistible harmony with the whole of God's creation.

St Clare of Assisi tells the same story, but in different images and in more subtle ways. She, too, leads us to that place where we find our fullest satisfaction, in gazing on, looking at, contemplating Christ. In her beloved San Damiano, she put down her anchor and found the whole of creation, the overflowing full embrace of God's love. Like Francis, a key to her journey was the radical search for simplicity. She fought tenaciously to defend her Holy Poverty, for she knew that any compromise led quickly to a heart too cluttered to receive the fullness of God's love.

Sister Frances Teresa tells these intertwined stories with a freshness of expression and a clarity of insight. Her account will appeal to all those who feel dissatisfaction with their day-to-day living, or who have a deep instinct that the true riches of life have so far eluded them. But readers must be ready for a challenging time, for Francis and Clare lived life to the full, with all the radical implications of the Gospel.

The story told here is compelling. If we let it, it will stir us to attempt to follow the same joyful road.

VINCENT NICHOLS
Bishop in North London

Introduction

When it began, this book was to have been focused on people in that uncomfortable transitional stage between saying prayers and contemplative prayer. As I worked on it, however, I realised that because our relationship with God and our daily lives are so inextricably one, I needed to cast my net much wider, and to catch other fish than that single, if important, moment. I also knew from my own life and the lives of friends who have talked with me, that there is a need for something to be said about spirituality in times of stress. I knew, too, that much of what Francis and Clare experienced and said is still extremely relevant. In addition, I wanted to try to articulate that vision of community which was so fundamental to their lives, a community in which, because we are each the beloved of God, we are all brothers and sisters to each other and to all creation. I was, and am, convinced that this world-view, rooted as it is in the fidelity of God, offers guidelines which are pertinent to us today as we rethink how to live in our endangered and wonderful world. As well as all this, I would very much like to open a doorway for others to be enriched by all that Francis and Clare have to offer us. For these reasons, and because it is always better to read the book than books about the book, I have added some suggestions for further reading. I hope that some people, at least, may be encouraged to pursue their acquaintance with these two great human beings.

In the matter of prayer-as-such, Francis and Clare gave us no formal instruction, but a careful reading of their writings suggests that in their own experience they knew three basic modes of prayer, all of which were present all the time, although one or the other usually predominated. This suggested to me that these three modes could well be named conversion, contrition and communion, and that they have a concurrent as well as a consecutive nature. In one sense, it is obvious that the conversion of chapter 1 must precede the communion of chapters 8 and 9, but in another sense, without the vision of chapter 10 we may not have the motivation to survive the struggles of the earlier chapters. Conversion can only be begun again and again, beginning without end in St Gregory's words; like Francis on his death-bed saying, 'Let us now begin to serve God, for up to now we have done nothing.' As we remain sinners, so we remain in need of conversion and redemption, but sinners though we are, the closest union with the Godhead is offered us. If we do not move into it, it is because we are unable, not because God is unwilling, and the process of becoming able, becoming apt in Hamlet's sense, is a description of the work of contrition.

With all this in mind, the book has been subdivided into three sections, Conversion, Contrition and Communion, trusting that people will feel free to apply the well-tried spiritual principle of: if the cap fits, wear it. If something seems relevant and helpful, then it probably is, but if it seems incomprehensible, it should peacefully be left on one side, awaiting its turn. In our spiritual lives, which means in our lives, we are always turning and returning to God, always repenting, always learning how to live and pray, always one with God, always summoned beyond. Yesterday's puzzles form tomorrow's enlightenments.

There is a certain kind of spiral which strikes me as a good image of our journey towards God. It is, in fact, a straight line drawn on a sphere, a pleasing geometrical demonstration of God writing straight with crooked lines. The best explanation is to imagine standing near the Equator, at Entebbe airport perhaps, then getting into a plane and flying off in a north-easterly direction. If we fly steadily in this same direction we will, because the earth is a sphere, go round and round the globe in diminishing spirals until eventually our plane will stall and land heavily on the North Pole, a method of reaching God which some of us will recognise. Even if we had not intended to head towards it, our travelling will have been oriented by this north, this Pole will have been the determining factor deciding which way we were going and even which way up we were.

For many of us, our Christian living is very much like the course of that pilot; we ourselves may not know where we are, yet God still remains the Pole of all our travelling, and in the end, amazingly, our strange spirallings will lead us home. Francis and Clare, however, lived out another saying, that God is a sphere of whom the circumference is nowhere and the centre everywhere. For them, everywhere was north, and they drove to it as straight as an arrow to the bull's-eye. This is best summed up in Clare's own words: The Son of God has become our way and Francis shows it to us. Look at Christ, she says again and again. The stages of conversion, contrition and communion are simply ways of talking about the process of doing this, of isolating moments in that process and discussing what happens.

I have tried, where possible, to avoid personal pronouns for God, but have not embarked on using he/she or him/her, partly because it can be so irritating to read and partly because each is as wrong as the other, or: neither is more right than the other. Because I, personally, find it distracting to have the masculine and feminine pronouns changed from page to page, I have not done that either. The truth is that we need another pronoun for God and so far have not found one, and it seems better simply to say so than to embark on something which I feel to be contrived and unsatisfactory. In addition to that, of course, both Francis and Clare used masculine pronouns, so that it would have become even more complicated had I taken to using feminine ones. In the matter of translation, I have made my own of all Clare's writings and of Francis' 'Canticle of Creation', but for the rest, I am heavily indebted to Fr Regis Armstrong OFM, CAP for his work in this field and to the Franciscan Herald Press for collecting Franciscan source documents in the volume known as the *Omnibus of Sources*.

Finally, I would like to pay tribute to my own community where, for more than thirty years, I have been privileged to see Franciscan living put into practice. I would like to thank all those who encouraged and helped me, but especially Sisters Aelred, Pat and Francis Joseph, who read the book in typescript and who each made such different comments and criticisms, besides helping me with my tendency to tie myself in grammatical knots. I would also like to thank Bishop Vincent Nichols who did the same, rescuing me on the way from several theological temerities. If any now remain, they must have gone in later and the credit is entirely mine.

In conclusion, what better can one say than Clare's own

words of blessing to her sisters: May the Lord be with you
always and may you be with the Lord, always and in every
place.

For those not familiar with the lives of Francis and Clare, here
are a few biographical facts. A few world and Church events
are included (in italic) to help site Francis and Clare in context.

1170	*Death of Thomas à Becket at Canterbury*
1182	Birth of Francis
1190	*Death of Frederick Barbarossa*
1193/4	Birth of Clare
	These were the years of the Fourth Crusade, the founding of the Trinitarian Order, the Knights Hospitaller
1194	*Council of York*
1196	*Eleanor of Aquitaine dies*
1200	*Council of London*
	Clare and her family fled to Perugia with other families from the nobility at war with the Commune of Assisi. Francis took part in this war, on the other side, and was taken prisoner.
	Sung Dynasty in China
1206	Conversion of Francis
1208	Francis hears Matthew's Gospel read and is joined by his first companions
1209	The Pope approves Francis' Rule
1210	Clare first hears Francis preach
1212	Clare is dedicated to God in the Portiuncola chapel, on the evening of Palm Sunday, and finally settles at San Damiano
1215	Francis and Dominic attend the Fourth Lateran Council. Clare is persuaded to take the title of Abbess
1216	The Pope gives Clare the Privilege of Poverty, of 'possessing nothing'
1218	Clare's sister, Agnes, is sent to Florence as Abbess. 'Rule' of Hugolino imposed on Clare
1219	Francis goes to the Holy Land

1220	The first brethren are martyred in Morocco. In this same year the Poor Clare community in Rheims is founded, traditionally the first in France. *Fifth Crusade*
1224	Clare falls sick and Francis receives the stigmata on Mount La Verna
1226	Francis dies and is canonised in 1228. Celano writes his *First Life*. There are now twenty-four of Clare's communities in Italy, and the Order spreads to Spain
1228	*Sixth Crusade*
1229	*Carmelites come to Europe*
1231	Anthony of Padua dies
1234	Clare writes her first letter to Agnes of Prague, daughter of the King of Bohemia, who founds a monastery in Prague
1235	Clare's second (extant) letter to Agnes *Roman de la Rose written (approx. date). Mongol raids in Central Europe*
1237	Clare's third letter to Agnes
1240	Saracens attack San Damiano, saved by Clare
1241	Siege of Assisi raised by prayers of the sisters
1242	*The Sainte Chapelle (Paris) is built*
1240	*Cimabue born*
1245	*Council of Lyons*
1246	*Feast of Corpus Christi first celebrated in Liège*
1247	Rule of Innocent IV imposed on Clare who ceases to be obliged to the Rule of Saint Benedict
1248	*Seventh Crusade*
1252	Clare writes her Rule
1253	Clare's fourth and last known letter to Agnes August: Clare dies November: her sister Agnes of Assisi dies There are now over 150 communities associated with Clare *The Sorbonne (Paris) is opened*
1255	Clare canonised; Celano writes her life
1260	Clare's body and the community of San Damiano transfer to their present monastery of Santa Chiara within the walls of Assisi

PART I

Conversion

The Beginning of Conversion

The story is told of St Francis that one day he and his brothers came to a crossroads. Francis shut his eyes while the others spun round and round, and when he shouted 'Stop!' they went off, in whatever direction they were facing, to convert the world. This story is a neat image of the experience of conversion, for it, too, means coming to a crossroads where we go into an apparently random spin which, when it eventually slows to a halt, leaves us facing who knows where, except that the direction will radically affect the rest of our lives. Often our co-operation with grace will, at first, mean nothing more than surrender to spinning as an image of our surrender to God so that, for us as for the brothers, the direction we are to take can be made clear.

The word itself, conversion, has wandered down to us, through Italian and Latin, from an Indo-European root which conveys the idea of *becoming*. It is a word about a process, pregnant with life and new beginnings. It also embraces the meaning of worth, and the two notions come together to suggest that conversion is a process of realising our true worth. We are, strictly speaking, converted to good things, not to bad. Clare and Francis of Assisi both understood this and took conversion to mean setting off in the direction of God, a long journey to the farthest reaches of their being, a discovery of their true worth. As a result of this, conversion also included the repair of sin and the restoration of order, it meant responding to God and opening themselves to the great life of Christ.

None of this came any more naturally to them than it does to us, yet, because they tried to commit themselves simply and totally, they continued to spin before God until the direction became clear. In this, they are models for us, showing us what needs to be done and how to do it. They encourage us because, for all their innate greatness, we see them making the same mistakes that we make. We mark in them the familiar way in which we stumble around blindly and ignorantly, only realising years later that God was working through our apparently random spinning. It was just as difficult and just as simple for them as it is for us. There is no high road leading certainly to a gate called conversion; conversion is this apparently random spin in which, without knowing how, we find ourselves.

Francis' first biographer, the friar Thomas of Celano,[1] tells the story that towards the beginning of his conversion, Francis was so disorientated by fear of his father's anger, that he hid in a pit and only one person knew where he was. He hid there for a whole month, terrified and powerless. This friend brought him food which he ate in his hiding place, and everything he needed was stealthily rendered to him.[2] Francis' life was always highly theatrical, in a way which was both a gain and a loss for him. His inner drama was always real enough but sometimes, especially at the beginning, the external drama tended to obscure the inner reality, even from himself. With Clare it seems to have been the other way around; we sense that for her, the outer drama was the expression, not the catalyst, of the inner.

Nevertheless, what Francis acted out, dramatically and externally, many of us experience inwardly and less dramatically, and this is one of the reasons why he can still speak to us so clearly. Few hide in a pit for a month, but many of us go through periods of helplessness and impotence, times when the old ways no longer work and the new ways are not yet established. Many of us know periods when we feel paralysed with fears and uncertainties, anxieties and helplessness, and these prevent us from living out the values which we truly hold in our inmost hearts. Few of us feel that we are of the same calibre as Francis and Clare, but, in the end, each of us must be just as radically restored to God's eternal concept of us. We must all rediscover our original face and become who we were designed to be. This is our human calling, made more specific in our Christian calling, exemplified for us in Christ himself.

Both Francis and Clare discovered that this work, which God has initiated and seeks to complete, was something way beyond their wildest imaginings. For us, too, our greatest claim to fame is never anything of our own but rather that God has raised us to glory, and the attendant summons to conversion is because, in God's economy, glory means to serve. However mistakenly, we tend to feel quite ready for glory, but less ready for the kind of service which we learn from Jesus Christ. In the upside-down school of God's values, we will learn how love and service interact with glory and how, for us as for Christ, they will mean both death and resurrection. Francis' words, 'Who am I and who are you?' will make more and more sense to us. By the end of our spinning, which may be the end of our lives, everything will have been redefined and will have found its true position in reference to the God who is continually creating us.

This is not just the task of a few religious, contemplatives perhaps; it is the destiny of the human race. God's 'problem' is that he does not want us to turn to him through force or guile, for he seeks friends and lovers, not slaves. Our problem is not so much that we do not want to turn to God, as that we do not know how to. We feel ready to love but lack the art. God, who is skilled in a kind of spiritual judo, tenderly uses our own weaknesses to overbalance us, so that willy-nilly we surrender to the spin of events and in so doing, surrender to love. As time goes on we realise more and more how God has been leading us, sharing and shaping our lives, meeting our deepest needs.

While he was in the pit, Francis had his first experience of loss of control. He was finding what we all find, that even when we hear the voice of God, we are not always free enough to respond to it. Like Francis, we too discover that we need to do a novitiate or training or to undergo some formation, in order to become capable of a free response. This, the start of our inner quest, is our first motive for prayer and penance; it indicates a readiness for growth and a longing for peace.

God's call means that grace is already at work in us, but nothing will change unless we also act in response. The grace given is that of being able to act; our part is to do so, if only in the smallest and most symbolic of ways. It is we who choose and we who act, but our doing so is itself a sign of God's presence in our lives. As Augustine said: 'We therefore will, but God works in us so that we do will. We therefore act, but God works in us so that we do act.'[3]

Francis, before his pit experience, had taken to wandering

in remote places and having endless spiritual talks with a long-suffering friend (we are not told his name) and we get a picture of a man increasingly off-balance, stunned, caught up in huge swings of mood and almost unable to speak clearly and simply—so different from the mature Francis. He had begun to discover how hard it is to give up things one is accustomed to, and that things which have once entered the mind are not easily eradicated.[4] So he had gradually slipped back into some of the old ways, for he was, says Celano, 'flighty and not a little rash'. One night Francis had a dream which suggested how he could translate his finite ambitions into eternal ones, and from this moment on, the whole process of conversion began to bite. He quite lost touch with the swagger which had led him to sell his father's cloth or boast that he would marry the most beautiful bride of all, but for a long time, he was neither converted nor not-converted, he knew the disadvantages of both and the advantages of neither.

Much later in his life, he was to reflect on this quality of ambivalence, for he saw that we all have it. It is often revealed by the way we set up our own attempts to rescue ourselves, but in such a way that we are inevitably driven deeper into trouble. Unless we choose to accept God's rescue, we will almost certainly achieve the exact opposite of the freedom we believe we seek, for our inner conflict is being expressed by this shipwrecking of our self-designed rescue. Francis said that the dynamic which drives this ambivalence is that we do not sufficiently reflect upon the true nature of our glory. We seek glory, but we want to give it to ourselves, and we do not realise how trivial our own glory is, when compared with that which God has already bestowed on us. 'Be conscious of the wondrous state in which the Lord God has placed you, for He created you and formed you to the image of His beloved Son according to the body, and to His likeness according to the spirit' (cf. Gen. 1:26).[5]

For Francis, however, all this was still in the future. Meanwhile he was hiding in the pit, afraid and trembling, desperately praying for a strength and deliverance which seemed slow in coming. He had learnt by now that his own efforts were not enough, that the things which he tried to do under his own strength were, in some curious way, sterile. He had sold everything (all his father's cloth) and tried to give the money for the rebuilding of the church at San Damiano. The priest there (soon to join him as a brother) prudently refused to touch it. Had Francis hoped that selling the cloth would also free his father from his mercantile ambitions? If so, he was doomed to disappointment, for Pietro Bernadone continued as before, except that their relationship went from bad to worse and, as far as we know, the conflict between them was never resolved. This may have been partly because, in many ways, father and son were similar kinds of men, although their values were so opposed. Pietro Bernadone's life-script to Francis could well have been something like: Decide what you want and go all out for it; because this is what they both did, although they differed in the goal they sought.

Francis' time in hiding was an almost total retreat from life, literally back to the womb of Mother Earth. Slowly, in the darkness and confinement of that pit, some deep inner process worked itself out. It had originally been a flight in fear but it became something much deeper, and there is a sense in which, for each of us, life must sometimes return to the first chapter of Genesis and the symbolic story of creation out of chaos. This is like a return to the drawing board of Genesis chapter 1, where nothing exists but the massive fact of God, and our own original chaos, our native mess. It is a chrysalis condition when our elements return to soup and we have to be remodelled. We are intrinsically chaotic, primeval chaos is our raw material, we ourselves are the formless void, but out of that emptiness and confusion God creates the beauty and intricacy of the universe.

For us, there is pain and peace as we wait with two incompatibles: the infinite potency of God and our own paralysed potentiality. We long for the fullness of being, yet bare existence seems to be all that we can manage and even that is God's, apparently haphazard, gift. Our danger is that we always have a tendency to settle for less, to acquiesce in allowing our potential to remain unrealised. We so easily become enamoured of the charms of being passive and not responsible, but in fact, we cannot rest there if we are to grow and take our place in God's designs. In the same way, the inevitable moment came for Francis when the thrust towards life overtook the drift towards escape. As soon as the pit had done its work, the infinite joy of God began to flood into his chaos and everything began to be transformed: 'Though he was in the pit and in darkness, he was nevertheless filled with a certain exquisite joy of which till then, he had had no experience; and catching fire therefrom, he left the pit and exposed himself openly to the curses of his persecutor'[6] that is, his father.

In one of his essays, Kierkegaard suggests that the self is a synthesis in which finitude is the limiting factor and the infinite is the expanding factor. The creative voice of God, the expanding factor, pushes at the boundaries of our being, encouraging us towards the possible greatness within us. Meanwhile our growth is hindered by the limiting factor of our tendency to seek something finite, to prefer the static and comfortable. The self is the precipitate of these two factors. At our best, we transcend the limitations, our spin becomes a spiral and we break free from the pendulum swings of indecision in which so many of us, like Francis, become imprisoned. Our spiral, like the universe, can expand continually, and no one knows our limits because few reach them. St Teresa of Avila hazarded the guess that the human capacity for growth is almost infinite.

All this potential was thrusting at Francis' being as he emerged from his pit. He was still not out of trouble because all who saw him thought he had gone mad and threw stones at him. Hearing his son's name being shouted out, his father rushed into the street and dragged him home, where he shut him in the cellar to come to his senses. Pietro then went off on a business trip, almost as if he wanted to deny the whole episode, or as if he hoped that by shutting Francis up in a room and going away, then the whole problem which Francis had become would also go away.

Like us all, Francis was heir to his own family and his father's history, and he felt the need to free himself from the inherited assumptions of his home and background. We see him struggling to establish his sense of self. The conflict with his father would not have been so searing or so ferocious had Francis not assimilated many of Pietro's attitudes, and many of their battles came from Francis' attempts to act against his father's aggressive assumption that might is right and money is power.

What actually happened was that Francis' mother, Pica, set him free to pursue the goal he thought he wanted. Obviously Francis was still in some confusion, but Pica's role is clear enough. Just as she was his mother physically, so she now became his mother spiritually, releasing him to follow his own path wherever it might lead. We know very little about Pica, although there is a theory that she was a Frenchwoman, and certainly all his life her son spoke and sang in French in moments of joy and elation. At several points in his story, we find that Francis' way to transformation was facilitated by women. It was as if they enabled him to tap resources in his own depths such as his intuition, his non-rational creativity, or his imagination (he had several dreams which showed him the way forward). Out of the same instinct, he sought advice from Clare on more than one occasion, and here, right at the beginning, this same dynamic was acted out when he had to wait for his mother to give him freedom. These principles of growth will hold for us as well. It is often the non-rational elements in us which will point the way forward and become the dolphin on which we ride to freedom. We need to seek these creative or imaginative aspects of ourselves, particularly when life seems stuck or prayer appears (to us) to be sterile, boring or dead. We need the simpler approach of our intuitive selves with their original outlook. We discover, as Francis did, that once we have seen things in their new light, then we are already changed, because there is no way back to our earlier perspective. To have seen even the fringe of God's garment is to wish to see the divine face, because, in the greatest meaning of the word, God is addictive. To have been touched once by God, once to have glimpsed those wide horizons, is to have stepped on to a road which ineluctably leads us to just such a dismantling and recreating as Francis underwent; we spin and are redirected and the road is Christ.

For us, caught in the heart of this process, prayer is advent, prayer is waiting, prayer can be winter. Like the Jewish people, we know that the Messiah will come one day; like the Magi, we hope we are travelling to meet him; like Mary, we know he is coming to us. We may continue with familiar motions of prayer, to light our candle and gaze at our icon or crucifix and try not to check the movements of the clock, but in reality, we are awaiting the end of winter and the coming of our God.

Nothing can hasten this process which both Francis and Clare called conversion. For them, this total surrender of mind and heart was a life-long work. They used to talk about 'the beginning of my conversion' but never about 'since my conversion'. They used to look back with wonder at what God had done in their lives, and their main concern was always about how they should live, not about how they should pray. Prayer was for guidance and help with living. 'In the beginning of my conversion', said Francis, 'no one showed me how I ought to live but the Lord himself taught me.' Celano tells us that everything which happened to Francis was an example for us, to help us believe that such grace can come to ordinary people like us, that this grace and this help are for everyone. 'The hand of the Lord therefore came upon him and a change was wrought by the right hand of the Most High, so that through him an assurance might be granted to sinners that they have been restored to grace and that he might become an example to all of conversion to God.'[7] Note the tense: an assurance might be granted that we *have been* restored to grace — grace is not conditional upon good behaviour but rather it is grace which makes 'good behaviour' possible, it is a gift already freely given, we are already reconciled to God (*Exultet*, Easter Vigil). This is the good news.

The first, and most outstanding, person for whom Francis' example acted as an assurance was, of course, Clare. In worldly terms Clare had even more points in her favour than he had, for her family was definitely among the powerful and aristocratic ones of the city. They were wealthy with a wide extended family, and during Clare's childhood had been caught up in conflict with the rising merchant class of Assisi who had tried to seize power from the entrenched aristocracy. When Clare was very young the whole family had fled into exile in Perugia (all of thirty miles away). From this reversal they had so come about that they regained all their property and power in the city. Clare tells us that when she was about seventeen (in 1211 or 1212) 'after the highest Father of heaven, through his mercy and grace, had been so good as to enlighten my heart so that I could do penance, according to the example and teaching of our most blessed father Francis, I, with the few sisters whom the Lord had given me, freely promised him obedience. This was not long after his own conversion.'[8] She does not seem to have had a pit experience in the way that Francis did, which reveals something typical of them, that their experiences tended to be complementary and parallel, rather than copies of each other. Clare had her own symbolic death, every bit as radical and dramatic as Francis' month in the pit, but quite different. She left her family one night by slipping away through a rarely-used door. It seems that this door was blocked up, since the family was astonished, next morning, that she had managed to clear a way through it. Some scholars suggest that doors like this one, at the end of a narrow passage (and still to be found in a number of old Umbrian houses) came into their own during times of conflict, because they could easily be held by a few men against a large number of attackers. Others say that these doors were used only for the dead. This last has caught the imagination of Clare's biographers, although there are no contemporary sources which come down clearly in favour of either theory.

Certainly Clare's night escape was a kind of death; it was death to her family, death to her life of privilege, death to marriage (and at least one rejected suitor lived to give evidence at her Canonisation Process) and death to the security she had taken for granted. Instead, because she had believed in Francis as literally as he had believed in Christ, she had sold all her goods and her marriage dowry, and given the proceeds to the poor. One wonders how she managed this. She then went to Santa Maria degli Angeli, where Francis received her into his Order. This was one of the three tiny chapels he had repaired and now rented from the Benedictines for an annual basket of fish. Innocent III had just given Francis' Order his verbal approval, because although he had been aghast at the starkness of Francis' ideals, he had not dared to say that one cannot live the Gospel to the letter.

After receiving her into his Order at Santa Maria degli Angeli, Francis took Clare to San Paolo in Bastia, a Benedictine monastery which had recently (1210) been granted the right of sanctuary. The sources suggest, but do not explicitly say, that Clare lived there as a servant rather than as a would-be-nun. For one thing, in her opinion she had already entered Francis' Order, and also, what else could her angry family have meant by saying that she had 'disgraced her class'? This interpretation is supported by the way the nuns of San Paolo seem to have done nothing to help Clare when her angry family descended on the place to take her home. The privilege of sanctuary did not include the defence of it, apparently.

For the young girl this experience may well have been shot through with that exaltation which comes from starting to live out our ideals, when she was reaching for 'the heat of life in a

handful of dust', even while it must also have been a kind of
dying. Young people flourish on opposition, and they often
need that capacity in order to find their own path in life, and
Clare was probably no exception. Even so, as she confronted
her family and began, for the first time, to experience real
poverty and insecurity, that period of her life must have con-
tained considerable darkness and pain. Yet years later, writing to St Agnes of Prague when Agnes was at a similar stage in
her prayer journey, Clare's advice to her was: 'Be filled with a
remarkable happiness and a spiritual joy.'[9]

This is certainly her counsel to us. We find it difficult today
to be happy, and even more difficult to be happy without
feeling guilty about those who are not. Yet if the servants of
God do not preserve happiness, it will vanish from the earth,
and that cannot be right. Joy, Abbot Marmion used to say, is
the echo of God's life in us. Why do we pray, if not to come to
an experience of life different from the one we now know?
Long before we have consciously begun to seek God, we are
moved by an inner dissatisfaction and by the conviction that
things are surely meant to be better than this—whatever this
is. The inner thrust of dissatisfaction leads us to sit and wait
before God, hoping in his goodness. If all we feel is distracted
or bored, this is the very inner restlessness which, again and
again, has already exposed our poverty to us, and forced us to
struggle with our inability to speak with God. It is only by
staying with this pain and inability and inadequacy, that
redemption can begin to work in us. The reality of redemption
is always ours. When we stand courageously in the truth of
ourselves (bored, distracted, scattered) then this other truth,
that we are redeemed, will also emerge, if we wait for it. In our
relationship with God, waiting never means that nothing is
happening. Like the psalmist, though with less wonder and
more wryly, we recall that a thousand years are like an evening to God. Not having a thousand years, we are impatient to
'get on with it', but God, who made us, knows our time span.

Because this state of impotence is so painful for us, we seek
for methods, techniques or rules of thumb, to control our own
lives again. Sometimes indeed, techniques can help us, skills
of breath control or simple exercises to focus the attention and
still the mind, but sooner or later there must come a point
where all these friends will desert us and we will be left before
God with our naked struggle to communicate. The pain of our

desire to do so will also remain. We must wrestle with this, as Jacob wrestled with the angel and would not let it go until it blessed him. This struggle is all right, as boredom is all right, as any wrestling, any truth, is all right, because this inability to pray is the threshold of a new world where all our values will be overturned and our lives seriously disturbed.

Everyone is free at this stage to say No. It is an invitation which is being offered, not a royal command. The fact that we are invited implies that we have, perhaps unknown to ourselves, the capacity to respond, and it may well be that to refuse will be a denial of our own destiny, with all the accompanying pain. There will be pain anyway, it must be said, though God in his ruthless mercy will often measure out our dying to us in small amounts, at least until we become more used to this new way of living by dying, of resurrection through death.

Our Yes to God, and our Yes to our own future, come into play as soon as we let the control pass out of our own hands. We are invited by the words of the Gospel that the truth will set us free, to make an inner leap into the darkness of ourselves. The important thing now is to be silent and listen to the truth, to let the truth do whatever it will. To be at this stage of our prayer journey is to be at the confluence of two personal worlds, the first, one in which we prayed seriously enough, usually on occasions of our own choosing; the second, a world in which prayer is where we live and move and have our being. Such prayer is where we garner up our soul, and either live or have no life. We do not come instantly, or easily, to this, but the choices we have already made are now leading us to it. This prayer is a rooting of the incarnation in our lives, it is active and effective on God's part, silent and consenting on ours. God has, so to speak, adopted an unchanging attitude of communication with us and will, inevitably, speak to us. The word of the Gospel, which is Christ, is for everyone, always, and the process of our personal conversion is about hearing this word ourselves and about Christ dwelling as fully in us as he is in the Trinity.

This deeper prayer heralds the end of all our spinning and the beginning of the journey. It takes the form of a gradual removal of obstacles and prejudices, opening us up wherever we are closed. It is a journey to the place where we can say Francis' words: My God and my All, with increasing understanding of what we are talking about. It is about being invited into that dialogue between heaven and earth where Christ is Jacob's ladder. 'How great and how worthy of praise is this commerce', says Clare, [10] echoing St Paul (2 Cor. 8:9).

As we do, Francis began by using words like a mantra long before he had fully learnt their meaning. When he prayed through the night and so astonished his host, Bernard of Quintavalle, he was declaring his wish and his intent: 'God is my all', but also, 'I wish God were my all.' Years later, his union with God would culminate in that strange, seraphic vision of La Verna, which would leave him so steeped in Christ that he carried the wounds of Christ in his own body, and other people, at least, were no longer sure which was Francis and which Christ.

All this, however, was in the future. At the beginning of his conversion he was full of questions: What are you, the most high God? And what am I, a most vile worm? These questions accompany us too: What are you? What am I? We try our different answers, as Francis did, until we hear God's particular word to us. Doing so, we discover that it can be the hardest thing in the world to sit still and feel ourselves under the scrutiny of God, even of a God who loves us. We learn the pain of unspecified desire. The author of the *Cloud of Unknowing* says, speaking about this time in our lives: 'All your life now must stand in desire': we must learn to accept this peacefully, and he tells us to lift up our hearts and 'mean' God, that is, focus our intention on, but leave all activity to, God. 'You look on and let him alone', he says. Do not meddle, be content to unlearn all previous lessons, study to do nothing, gaze and contemplate. It is significant that this wise author calls his book the *Cloud of Unknowing*, rather than the 'Cloud of Not-knowing'. Habits of being in the know die hard with us, but they must be broken. Habits of assessing progress by productivity and results, our own or anyone else's, must be changed. We are being led into a place where other values operate and the most important moments in our day, the most productive moments of our lives, will be those few and far-between instants which the author calls 'atoms'. By this he means tiny fractions of time, so small as to be indivisible and almost incomprehensible. In such atom-moments, God will work this work in us, and all those 'living in the earth will be wonderfully helped'.

2

Out of the Pit

When Francis came out of the pit he emerged, in every sense, into the light, and began to move towards that atmosphere of springtime which has characterised him in the public mind ever since. Even while still in the pit, Celano tells us, he began to be filled with a certain exquisite joy of which till then he had had no experience; 'and catching fire therefrom, he left the pit'.[1] In spite of the scars of this experience, joy gave him courage as he entered upon another series of conflicts, involving a still more radical self-stripping and even further pain. The difference was that he now knew where he was going. His feet were set on the way and every attack only served to clarify his sense of direction.

The first thing he did was to go into the city of Assisi and try to tell everyone what had happened to him, in a way which is so typical of us all when we are smitten with the fervour of a new conversion. Like us, he imagined that all he had to do was to tell people what had happened to him and they would immediately leave all and follow. He sincerely thought he was inviting them to follow God, but it is not so easy to eradicate our desire for recognition or our taste for telling others what they ought to do. This is what Milton felt, when he wrote of the early days of the Commonwealth: 'The glory of reforming all our neighbours was ours',[2] and we can smile, recognising it for what it is.

Francis arose, active, eager and lively; and, bearing the shield of faith to fight for the Lord, armed with great confidence, he took his way to the city. Aglow with a divine fire, he began to accuse himself severely of laziness and cowardice. When those who knew him saw this, they compared what he was now with what he had been; and they began to revile him miserably. Shouting that he was mad and demented, they threw mud and stones at him.[3]

The strange and eccentric is always frightening. We like our saints best when they are clean and tidy and dead. We do not like the process of liberation from convention which might lead us, or others, into bizarre actions, and we are not always sympathetic to the swings of behaviour which mark those undergoing change. This experience of being rejected and stoned revealed to Francis one of the first consequences of the Gospel, namely that, sooner or later, we will be challenged to put God before all else, that the pearl of the Kingdom is buried and hidden and that the price of finding it is high. Francis had no idea, at that time, what this was to entail or where it would lead him.

The first place it led him was to the Bishop's palace and to a confrontation with his father who was angrily demanding back everything he had ever given to this son, now the source of such embarrassment for the family. This confrontation was the famous occasion when Francis stripped off all his clothes and handed them back to his father, saying that from now on he would only say 'Our Father' to his Father in heaven. It was a definitive break with his past, a radical uprooting. It was also somewhat aggressive and confrontational, and the mature Francis would probably have handled it quite differently. We get the impression that the old man's heart broke over this conflict with Francis, for it appears that Francis had been the favourite son. There was one other brother at least, Angelo, a shadowy figure, who poked fun at Francis whenever they met, but who in no way measured up to the stature of his brother. At one time the situation became so bad that Pietro Bernadone would curse Francis whenever he saw him, and Francis hired a beggar to follow him round and counteract the curse with a blessing.

The next thing that happened to Francis was that he fell among thieves. Robbers attacked him one day as he wandered through the woods,

singing praises to the Lord in the French language. When they asked him in a ferocious tone who he was, the man of God replied confidently in a loud voice: I am the herald of the great King! But they struck him and cast him into the ditch filled with deep snow, saying: Lie there, foolish herald of God! But he rolled himself about and shook off the snow; and when they had gone, he jumped out of the ditch and, glad with a great joy, began to call out the praises of God in a loud voice throughout the grove.[4]

Ironic to be robbed when he had just embraced poverty, he who would have been so worth robbing a few months earlier! Clearly his health and vigour are returning for he simply shakes off the snow like a young dog and trots on. After this, he worked for a time as a kitchen hand in a nearby monastery, but he was treated so badly that he was forced to leave. He obviously received the contemporary treatment meted out to the insane and found it beyond human endurance. He was given nothing to wear, not even an old garment, and had to subsist on what scraps of food he could scrounge, although the abbot later apologised when he discovered that Francis was not mad but holy.

These events, his breach with his father, his attack by robbers, his service and bad treatment in the monastery, were like stations, focal points along his journey into freedom. We have to remember what Francis had been: leader of the city's youth, fastidious, elegant, expensive, charming and talented. He had been the darling of Assisi, his name known to almost everyone, popular and ambitious, with every reason to expect those ambitions to be realised. Now his name was forbidden in his father's presence, the people of Assisi thought him mad and threw stones at him, robbers tossed him around like a joke, monks who would once have welcomed him as a postulant treated him so harshly that 'all pity was withdrawn from him'. Through it all, Francis matured as a joyful man. At first there was something euphoric, almost high, about him; even the encounter with Pietro before the Bishop had an intoxicating radicality. As the story unravels, however, the joy deepens and mellows, it becomes more spiritual and more grateful and less euphoric. In the beginning, he was the herald of a great king and all the glory of God was his glory too. In the end, he was an unprofitable servant, grateful for another day in which to begin to serve his Lord.

Not a moment of this colourful journey was to be lost, not because Francis made no mistakes but because God wasted nothing. With each event, Francis' awareness of God's call grew clearer. One day he was going along the road and there came into his mind the memory of a particularly deformed and ugly woman in the city. The idea took hold of him that if he carried on in the way he was going, then that was how he would end up. He was a young man who loved beauty and grace and elegance, to be ugly and loathsome would be a hard and bitter thing for him, but he prayed for the grace to be open to whatever came, even this. He discovered, as we do, too, that when we have been confronted with more than we can manage, God does not say: There, there, and take it all away. Rather, Francis' prayer was accepted, his generosity honoured. He was assured that the worst probably would happen and that his deep fears were accurate intimations of challenges to come. At the same time he was shown (as we are) that it was not as far beyond him as he imagined, but rather, as always with God, everything was possible even if it was also quite different from what he had anticipated. With the companionship of God even death is shot through with life. Like Paul, Francis had to learn that he really could do all things in the God who strengthened him.

From now on in our journey, we, like Francis, will move more and more into unknown territory. We will shift between moments of love for God and moments in which any kind of prayer seems quite impossible, even distasteful. It may even seem to us that in pursuing us and inviting us, God is also making life impossible for us. We become confused, or more confused. We may become, like the spinning friars, a little dizzy. We are entering the land of paradox and must not be surprised if we lose our bearings, because our old values are being overturned and the new ones are not yet in place. As a result, our sense of direction deserts us; we feel unsure about how to proceed, like a caterpillar at the end of a leaf, feeling blindly round for another leaf to walk on. This sense of not knowing where to go, is only resolved as we start to move along the Way of God. Until then, we are indeed in the wilderness and at the mercy of our own particular wild beasts, and we need to recall here that Christ, too, underwent a similar experience, and that it is by no means aimless or fruitless. It is the moment between the end of spinning and the start of journeying. One of the consequences of being lost in the wilderness is exactly this change of direction. This is why illness is often a factor in a conversion, because our inner confusion expresses itself in physical illness, which in turn forces us to

live differently and with changed values. In the course of this
change, our inner compass can become so confused that we no
longer even know where we want to go. We only know that
there is no way in which we can live our future as we have
lived our past. This can be a most searing experience of dis-
orientation and we are radically marked simply by enduring
it. It alone can be enough to make us ill.

Another characteristic of the wilderness experience is that
while it lasts it can seem to allow no room, no mental space,
for prayer. Prayer can seem quite impossible, largely because
of our overwhelming confusions, but also because of an apparent absence of God. God, it seems, is not in the wilderness.
This is because God *is* the wilderness and we are lost in it, an
experience both wonderful and terrible; and because wonder
and terror are neither of them feelings with which we can live
in any degree of comfort, we unconsciously seek rest in a
complementary feeling of bleakness about our whole situation.
Very often, people feel that they should be different before
they can pray, instead of remembering that it is prayer which
makes us different. We forget that God is in whatever is,
including ourselves. We must start, and can only start, from
where we are, and it may be a very subtle escape to keep
saying to ourselves that we cannot possibly start (or continue)
to relate to God from *this* place, let us wait until things are
different. It is part of our sin that we are so brilliant at making
excuses for not meeting God today.

> O that today you would listen to his voice,
> Harden not your hearts

pleads the psalmist (Ps. 95:7). In fact, of course, we are
already in relationship with God simply by existing, but we
are being invited to deepen this relationship. Sometimes, it
feels as if our existence is about all we can manage to give, and
at the end of prayer, the most we can say is that at least we did
not go and do something else. If we have stayed there, if we
have been physically present, honestly struggling to be present in mind and heart, especially in heart, then that is a great
deal. St Ignatius said that at such times, it is a good idea to
prolong the time of prayer rather than to shorten it. To settle
to pray for half an hour and then to stay on for another ten
minutes, is much wiser than to give up in despair after twenty
minutes. We will find that God has touched us, in spite of

everything. At the time we knew we were alone and nothing happened and the minutes went on for ever; yet we will look back later and see the careful way in which God had fitted our journey to our needs, sensitively demonstrating that no two people make the same journey, no two people go through the same 'stages' in the same order.

Some people feel that they do not go through any stages at all but remain in a kind of heavy limbo for years, in which nothing much exists except the burden of being themselves. This can be a long wilderness and a hard one. At such times people need encouragement to keep going. Indeed, most of us need someone to remind us that God is always creative and loving and that that includes us. If we are doing all we are able, or all that, at present, we see to do, then we must rest as peacefully as possible in things as they are. This may be all we *can* do but it is also all we *need* to do. We so easily slip into thinking that the goodness of God is for the rest of humanity but not for me. This is quite a mistake; every minute of our long apparent delay in the wilderness is the tender work of his love. However, it is sometimes the case that there are aspects of our lives which do need to change before we can go any further. We may be keeping ourselves in prison, since, on the whole, we forge and maintain our own chains. At this point we may need to make an honest assessment of ourselves, and this will be helped by some simple questions such as: What are the handful of things for which I would die? What are the handful of things without which I cannot live? These questions, like the light upon the scaffold, help to concentrate the mind. They pare away the multiple irrelevances of life and expose its bones to our view. This helps us discover where we really want to go because one thing is sure—we shall go there, for good or ill. On the whole, we do what we want to do.

Celano tells us that God showed Francis the way forward at just such a time, by saying into his heart: Take the bitter for the sweet; despise yourself if you wish to acknowledge me.[5] Despise yourself: the word means literally, to look down upon, and so in its profoundest meaning, to see ourselves from a different point of view. The usual meaning, of scorn, has no place here, while to value ourselves as nothing only has a place in the context of being lovingly given, so that care for ourselves is now God's business. As we saw earlier, to be nothing really means to be God's raw material. In our damaged condition, we have a tendency to write ourselves off, we assume that to be nothing means to be of no value, but in fact, rightly despising ourselves only means that we shift ourselves away from the centre of the universe. We make a great mistake by engaging in a contest with God for the centre stage, not because God querulously demands it, but because God is the Centre. The two words signify the same thing. There is a medieval saying, variously attributed, that God is a sphere, of which the circumference is nowhere and the centre everywhere. It is quite impossible for us to be, or to be at, the centre. To see this is rather like Copernicus' experience when he positioned the sun at the centre of the solar system and suddenly, there the planets were, elegantly sailing on an ellipse of great beauty. All the complicated mathematics needed to explain their gyrations had now become superfluous. As so often, the simple solution is the most beautiful, and beauty is a test of truth.

Francis discovered, as we do, that his journey into freedom meant that he himself had to expand so as to measure up to his expanding horizons. He was taught progressive lessons in self-giving and his adventures quickly brought him specific and relevant chances to practise it. We are told that he found lepers so horrible that he would only look at their houses from a safe distance of two miles, holding his nose with his hands.[6] One day as he went along the road, however, he met an actual leper who held out a begging hand to him. Without giving himself time to think, Francis gave him money and kissed him. When later, he turned to look back, there was no leper to be seen. Fearful lest it had been just a one-off triumph, he clinched it by doing the same thing again at the next opportunity, and then he went to the leprosarium itself and gave money to each of the lepers there, along with his kiss. 'Thus he exchanged the bitter for the sweet and manfully prepared himself to do the rest.'[7]

A lot of speculation has gone on in Franciscan circles about the significance of this kiss of the leper, particularly as the leper vanished, leading the pious reader to conclude that it had been Christ in disguise. In a certain sense, this is certainly who it was, for Christ himself declared that whatever we do to one of his little ones, we do to him; in this sense the leper Francis kissed was indeed Christ. On another level, the leper was also Francis' own self, his despised and neglected self, the putrefying and decaying aspects of his personality, all his as-yet unredeemed areas. The leper was that part of himself which Francis preferred not to know about and kept hidden away, unacknowledged and never approached. 'He would go no nearer than two miles and hold his nose.'

We are touching here on an extremely important principle of spiritual and psychological life, namely that acceptance is the gateway to change. When Francis accepted the leper, not just in words but by his profoundly symbolic act of loving welcome, by his kiss that is, the leper disappeared because, by definition, a leper is an outcast. Once he or she has been accepted, the leper-condition is cured. The man may still be sick, but that is another matter. This act of self-acceptance is one of the hardest things, and in struggling to make it we are confronted by all the distinction between simple and easy. To kiss our leper is the simplest gesture in the world; it might also be the hardest, but until we do take our leper to our hearts we are always travelling with an aspect of our lives to which we must give a two-mile clearance. Constantly to be skirting an issue, as Francis skirted the leprosarium, is the quickest way to lengthen a short journey.

God's word to Francis was: Take the bitter for the sweet. He does not say that the bitter will become sweet, although it sometimes does. What is being recommended here is that we act out of God's values even though they are not yet ours on the level of our feelings. Let the bitterness of a thing, God says, stand as a cipher for sweetness; do not be put off by feelings of distaste, which are like a litmus test revealing what is still unredeemed in us. This is not an exhortation to become a doormat to the world, but a hint that our reactions have something to tell us about ourselves. The bitterness is a merciful revelation, telling us that we are still angry, proud, resentful, revengeful and so on. God is not saying that if it hurts, it must be good for us, but that to kiss our leper is to open our hearts. When we do this, we are most God-like, bringing joy to ourselves and those around us.

By accepting this reversal of our values, we surrender ourselves to the unknown. The Gospel is full of advice to do just this: Lose your life in order to save it, take up your cross and follow me, leave your family and discover your neighbour, set out on a journey with no provisions. Choose the bitter, God advises Francis, choose freely what must be. Instead of being constrained and imprisoned by circumstances, begin to discover freedom even within situations which you do not like and cannot change. Godly living is a learned skill, and like all skills is perfected by practice. If we wait until we feel like it, we shall never enter our leprosarium, never meet our leper, never come to that particular awareness of the sacred which can only be found by embracing reality. God is in what is—including the leper within. So we come full circle: the leper is us, and the leper is Christ.

From the moment of that liberating kiss, Francis began to live in Christ in a new way, he became free and began to exercise his restored creativity. In the most literal sense, he began to build. Celano, who had pondered deeply on the inner meaning of Francis' acts, says:

> The first work that blessed Francis undertook when he had gained his freedom . . . was to build the house of God. He did not try to build one anew but he repaired an old one, restored an ancient one. He did not tear out the foundation but he built upon it, ever reserving to Christ his prerogative, though he was not aware of it, for other foundation no one can lay, but that which has been laid, Christ Jesus.[8]

He did for the churches what God had done for him. Learning from God's way of working, he was careful to restore the superstructure on the foundations which were already there, preserving the good and repairing the damaged. He saw that God had given him a blueprint for all action: in himself, in others, on the building site, in his mission. He realised that the foundation which had already been laid in him was Christ Jesus himself; laid first by the simple fact of our shared humanity, because God had created and formed us to the image of his beloved Son according to the body, and to his likeness according to the spirit.[9] For us, house of God as we are, as for San Damiano and the other little churches which Francis repaired, our restoration and redemption mean being re-established after a period in ruins. This can be both the wider ruin in which all humanity is implicated, or more personal ruin, unique to us.

We remain on the same foundations, because we will always be unalterably ourselves as God created us, but we must not lose sight of the fact that restoration is only the first stage. When we are restored, then like San Damiano we are made ready for a new destiny and a new future. 'Ladies will live here who will give glory to our heavenly father by their way of life.'[10] Through welcoming God into our partially restored house, we become the church, that is, the sacred space where God is worshipped. Worship, 'acknowledge Me', can begin when we are no more than a husk of a house, even a ruin, there is no need to wait for all the furnishings. Worship itself will bind our stones together and make us whole. Worship will give us integrity, that is, the new virginity towards which we are being led, a virginity of completion and wholeness, the mark of the new creation. This is a given, not an achievement; least of all is it a physical condition which we have, or have not, retained.

Like the sacraments themselves, this image of us as a church is not only a symbol but it also brings about what it symbolises. It is not only the image of us as the house of God, it also helps us to become the home of God. We have to learn how to live as God's temple and often we start awkwardly, as Francis did when he began by literally building with stones, but at the same time he was taking his first, tentative steps towards living this new vision. As we have seen, one of the four little churches which he repaired was San Damiano where Clare was later to live, and it was there that he heard the words 'Francis, repair my church,' which were to become the foundational command for his future Order: 'Do you not see that my house is falling into ruin? Go, and repair it for me. Francis, repair my church.'

Like Francis, we too go through a novitiate in God's service, during which we make mistakes, misunderstand and swing from one extreme to another. Like Francis, we experience the paradox that God makes us whole yet leaves us wounded. Like Francis, we learn that prayer is not so much the words we say as the way we live. Our meetings with God, no matter how brief and tentative, will certainly leave us changed if we open ourselves to them in all honesty, but this honesty must also embrace what we do when we come from prayer and mingle with others.

Brother Angelo, one of Francis' earliest companions and probably the author[11] of the *Legend of the Three Companions*, tells us that as a result of these experiences, Francis was 'so changed as to make him appear a different man.'[12] He even looked different, physically, and although they did not understand it, his companions could quite clearly see it. Looking back later, they realised that even then the broad outlines of his vocation were clearly to be discerned although, at the time, none of them understood what they were seeing.

We, too, when we look back over the years, will see that there has been steady growth, although we cannot discern it now. Perspective brings vision. There is also a curious grace which is sometimes given to us when we reflect and throw glances back over our shoulder at our own story, and that is that even though our day-by-day lives can seem over-full, over-crowded, noisy and not at all prayerful in the way we dream about, yet, looking back on the years, or even just the months, they do seem to be full of God. They can even seem to be full of exactly the sort of prayer, deep, unitive, loving and quiet, which we have longed for but sadly concluded may never be given to us. It is as if we have had our hearts desire and had not noticed.

A Place in which to Pray

Let us now see what we can learn from Francis and Clare about the actual mechanics of praying. Let us see if we can learn more about what we can do to help ourselves when we take that step of physically moving apart from our daily affairs and settling down 'to pray'. What did they do?

Francis often began with what was later called a 'composition of place', but being Francis, he did not just do this in his mind, but acted it out and made physical places for prayer. He said, quite truly, that having a special place for prayer was a help because we are so vulnerable to distraction. There are any number of islands, rocks, mountains and caves which were all places where Francis used to go apart and pray because he had discovered that they helped him turn towards God. When he rested his eyes on the beauty which God had made, he was lifted up to God's own beauty. Creation was like a mirror for him, and in it he saw reflections of the One whom he desired, the Country towards which he travelled. At the same time, he was well aware that we only need a special place in which to pray because we are weak and imperfect. God fills everywhere, and in our prayer life we will be led slowly forward until, at least on occasions, this knowledge becomes experience as well.

Until then, because we are still vulnerable to distraction, we can be helped, as he was, by a 'place in which to pray'. If we can find somewhere out of doors or make a small and simple prayer corner indoors and, according to our fancy, light a candle, keep fresh flowers there, spread a prayer mat, and if we can also keep our daily muddle from overflowing into it, then this place will become a focus for us. Through the simple act of turning towards it, we will be re-rooted in the experiences of inner silence which we have known there. If (which is highly likely) we are still distracted, we must peacefully bring that distracting matter into our prayer itself, because it is our life we are offering to God, not our perfect performance. In reality, there are no distractions for a God who is everywhere, so we can afford to let every by-way wind back to its true beginning, and every straying thought become a window on to God. The clear message of the Incarnate Christ is that all human life is material for discussion with the Lover of all that lives.

The second simple aid to prayer is to give it time: to spend regular time doing it, as well as to allow time for the cumulative effects of prayer to reveal themselves. The hour at which we pray will inevitably govern the content of it. Prayer in the morning may be filled with our hopes and fears for the day or it may be much less invaded than prayer at night. This, after a day's work, will reflect our tiredness and may be flooded by people we have met and things that have happened. All these can be brought to God and discussed. Wounds, tiredness, reasons for thanksgiving, signs of God at work in our lives, things we are worried about, trivial and major, matters for which we need even more help or forgiveness, areas of disaster, the anguish of human life, all are the raw material of prayer. Francis used to ask the Lord quite practical things about what would be good for his new Order, or what he should do in this or that situation, but the heart of prayer was always his worship of God, the other was but the prologue.

Francis would often approach prayer by asking himself two questions: What is God? What am I? These two questions helped to site him in reality, his own and God's. In this way he cleared his mind of daily debris, and focused himself once more on God. His many answers to his own question have come down to us like a glorious list of what God is: holy, almighty, strong, great, good, love, charity, wisdom, beauty, peace, joy, justice, moderation, all riches, meekness, refreshment, hope, sweetness, life. If we repeat these phrases slowly and prayerfully: You are love, You are wisdom, You are all our riches, then we will begin to learn the art of worship as Francis learnt it. Francis was quick to see God in the everyday things, quick to see that each everyday thing was God's gift to him, every beginning a most special gift. He used to say that we should particularly praise God when the sun comes up in the morning, because of ourselves we are blind people and the Lord has provided light for us. Francis loved the sun and the

light, explaining that Brother Sun has a greater resemblance
to God than any other creature. All physical light revealed to
Francis how God cares for us, so that by day and by night we
are given enough light for our journey, Brother Sun by day
and Brother Fire by night. Years later, when he was almost
blind and could not bear the light at all because of his eye
disease, he composed the Canticle of Creation in order to
celebrate the creation's glory and, above all, to celebrate

> His Excellency the Sun (our brother);
> through him you flood our days with light.
> He is so beautiful, so radiant, so splendid,
> O Most High, he reminds us of you.

To the second question, What am I? he would reply: A most
miserable worm. This opened his heart to a brief awareness of
his own need and the long realisation of all that God had done
for him. Francis was so steeped in Scripture that the words of
the Bible lie behind almost all his own words. Here, too,
behind such a phrase as 'a most miserable worm' lie God's
compassionate words in Isaiah to Jacob, his poor worm,
whom he will raise up:

> Do not be afraid, Jacob, poor worm,
> Israel, puny mite.
> I will help you — it is Yahweh who speaks —
> the Holy One of Israel is your redeemer.[1]

This phrase 'a most miserable worm' was far from being a sick
self-abasement for Francis. Rather it was a kind of shorthand
in which he summed up his creation out of nothing, his sense
of great present need and the whole story of God's love for
him. It was an affirmation of trust in the one who had promised to help him. Francis felt he had shared Mary's experience, that God had looked on him in his lowliness and honoured him. He understood that his ineptitude and poverty
were the very things which formed his passport to grace.
Francis' concept of himself as being more needy than anyone
else was no false humility. In the blackness of the pit, he had
most thoroughly explored what was in him and what he was
truly like, and he never forgot the lessons he learnt there. It
was precisely because he had entered so deeply into his own
darkness that the light was able to flood his whole being, as if
this journey into his own hinterland had opened it up to grace

and joy. During that painful journey he had been most literally converted, turned around, until he had left all self-seeking behind and sought only God. Surely part of what touches us in Francis is this uncomplicated and enviable delight in God, which enabled him to say things like: Isn't it wonderful that the Lord wanted people to exist who would be happy to have nothing but his most high and glorious Self!²

Clare approached her prayer in a very similar way to Francis and obviously learnt how to pray from him. In their evidence at the Canonisation Process, the sisters speak of 'when she returned from prayer', suggesting that she, like Francis, went apart to pray—though how she managed in the narrow confines of San Damiano with a community of forty or fifty sisters, remains unexplained. Clearly it sometimes happened that her prayer extended itself in time, so that she was, relatively speaking, absent for some while. When she came back, they tell us, her face used to shine, and she, who was always gentle, would speak with even greater tenderness than usual.

What did she do in her time at prayer? What would she recommend for us? She gives us one fundamental bit of guidance: Look at Christ. Francis gazed into the mirror of creation and saw Christ; Clare gazed into the mirror of Christ and saw eternity. She tells us: Place your mind in the mirror of eternity. By gazing into this mirror of eternity, we see how to live in time. 'Gaze upon him, think about him and contemplate him, if you want to imitate him.' Clare understood this imitation of Christ to mean something far more radical and searching than merely keeping the law; it meant becoming like Christ by doing what Christ did, that is, gazing into the depths of the Godhead.

> Place your mind in the mirror of eternity!
> Place your soul in the splendour of glory!
> Place your heart in the icon of the divine substance!
> Through contemplation be completely transformed
>   into the image of the Godhead itself.³

By gazing into Christ, the mirror, we see eternity; in other words, by gazing into Christ we see God. In fact, this gazing means being caught up into the life of the Godhead itself. From Christ, we learn how to live in God. If Francis saw all creation caught up into God, Clare saw the same vision from

the other side, that God has flooded into everything, that
God, through Christ, is inextricably involved with humanity,
indeed with all creation.

It was one of her key ideas that because of the incarnation,
because God had become human in Christ, our union with
God is not only bound to be fruitful, but our fruitfulness, like
that of Christ, is for now, for this world. It is not something we
vaguely hope for in another life. 'In the field of the world
and in human hearts, God has hidden a treasure without
comparison.'[4] The treasure is in the field of the world and in
human hearts. Our glory and our truest creativity are to find
that hidden treasure. This is a deeply life-affirming perspective and completely typical of Clare. For her, our task and our
glory are to bear Christ in the present moment, with all the
consequences of transformation which will follow. 'As the glorious Virgin of virgins carried Christ physically, so you, without any doubt, will contain him spiritually.'[5] 'To use the very
words of the Apostle himself, I judge you to be a co-worker of
God and one who supports those members of his Body who
are giving way.'[6] It is our Christian task to bear Christ and
support each other, and she contrasts it rather dramatically
with 'certain much mistaken kings and queens of this world,
who allowed their pride to reach the skies and their heads to
top the clouds — in the end they become a heap of manure.'[7] So
much for Frederick Barbarossa, one-time suitor of Agnes of
Prague, her correspondent!

In general, the spirituality of Francis and Clare was so
loving and encouraging and full of light because it was rooted
in the great deeds of God. It was a spirituality of salvation
leading to union. They saw the heights of glory and union
being offered to everyone, not because we are fit for it (union
with God, as we have said, is not the reward of good
behaviour) but as a gift, a work of unimaginable love. God not
only loves us but also likes us. Since they knew that there were
no limits to the goodness of God, they could take such a
wonderfully positive attitude and know it to be realism; they
thoroughly understood that Christ, having once become what
we are, remains united to us forever and as a result, all the
universe is transformed.

Images of Christ fill Clare's letters: Christ the Liberator,
the King, the Light, the suffering Lover; above all, and most
original of all, Christ the Mirror. Looking into this Mirror we

see what God created us to be, and what we are called to become. Just as we cannot deny or ignore the pain of humanity, so we must come, sooner or later, to gaze into the passion of Jesus, if we would gaze long into the mirror. In his passion, we see something of what we have made of ourselves, humanity as God sees it, suffering and dying. Then we will begin to touch the edges of his pain and to discover what Julian of Norwich meant when she said that if he is in pain then we are in pain, if we are in pain then so is he, because of our shared nature. This sharing of pain changes our lives far more effectively than any decisions we might make out of strength of character. The minute we open our hearts to the pain of Christ, which is the pain of the world, then our values begin to be altered, and we with them. Through these wounds of Christ, we look into the heart of God. In Christ, what we are, that is, sinful and human, interacts with what he himself is, that is, God; as if he silvered the clear glass of his divinity with our opaque humanity to become a mirror for us to look into.

Clare knew well that when we gaze at someone for a long time with an open heart, then love is generated in us. God is certainly no exception to this. To see Christ is, as he himself said to Philip, to see God. To have seen the beauty of God in Christ is to be led to love God. What Clare recommends to us is a prolonged exposure to the eternal, precisely by gazing at Christ. Christ is the way, she said, and Francis showed it to me. We walk this way by contemplating Christ, which means looking at him in such a way as to see deeply into his mind, exactly as we might peer into a mirror. He, in Clare's words, is the icon, or image, of the Godhead, and to gaze at Christ is the beginning, middle and end of all prayer. Peering into this mirror of eternity will lead us into the splendour of glory; then, just as to be in the sun makes us warm, with a faint echo of the sun's tremendous heat, so to be in the presence of God makes us good, with a faint echo of God's tremendous goodness. When our being is flooded by God, Clare goes on, 'you will hold him by whom you and all things are held together'.[8]

Through the years Clare learnt, from her own and others' experience, that the desire to imitate Christ is the first stage of doing so. The next stage comes when, as a result of our looking at Christ, our lives begin to fall into Christ-like patterns. This happens when we 'gaze upon him, consider him, contemplate him'.[9] These three verbs describe three stages in this process of prayer.

We gaze upon him when we read the Gospels and see what he said and did, what happened to him, what impact he had on those around him. This is a search for information; it includes study and spiritual reading as well as simply looking. In another place she recommends us to pay attention to the external elements of Christ's life, to observe them and take note.

To consider him is to reflect and ruminate, to ponder prayerfully on what we have read. If spiritual reading is food, then this is the process of taking it in, digesting it and making it our own. Clare is leading us from the experience of looking, on to the deeper experience of pondering and studying. We are being led away from the informative and the sensory, to reflect in our hearts on the life of Christ, to wonder at what he did and what happened to him. We should mull it over, she is telling us, let it sink in, and allow ourselves to be drawn deeper.

We will then be brought *to contemplate him*, which means to sit and be steeped in this God with whom we have been reconciled in Christ. We will learn that this is God's work, not ours. Contemplating means allowing ourselves to be changed, as distinct from working to make ourselves different. It includes wonder, awe, tenderness, amazement; it means bewilderment and confusion; it includes wasting time and doing nothing; it means simply being there, without thoughts or ideas, words or resolutions, sometimes even without feelings. It includes staying there with a painful sense that nothing is happening. It means realising our own nothingness and experiencing the pain of our emptiness. It includes resisting an almost permanent temptation to 'do something'. Not one moment of this time is wasted or lost, because each moment is a series of lessons on how to be human. Out of our steadfast looking at Christ will spring true love, because, in the words of Thomas Traherne, we are as prone to love as the sun is to shine; we have forgotten this comforting and wonderful truth, and long ago lost confidence in our essential goodness.

By this programme, then, under the threefold heading of gaze, consider, contemplate, Clare is leading us step by step into the heart of God. We are guided from external events into the meaning of those events and so into love. Our gaze is increasingly turned away from ourselves as we learn to look into the heart of this mirror where we see *ineffabilem caritatem*,[10] the love which cannot be told, even in fable and legend. We see our own past, too, in a new light and begin to gain a deeper insight into our lives. Then, she goes on to say, throw your whole being into this mirror, place your mind, heart and soul in it, and there be mysteriously transformed into just such an image of the Godhead, become an icon or presence of God in the world.

Clare also gives a vivid and, quite by chance, an extraordinarily modern, twist to this image, when she suggests that Christ is like a huge mirror hung beside the road. 'This mirror, hung on the wood of the Cross, urged all those who passed by it, to consider, saying: All you who pass by the way, look and see if there be any sorrow like my sorrow.'[11] She develops this metaphor by explaining how we can look into different parts of this mirror and see different aspects of Christ's life—as it were different parts of the road, for our Way is Christ himself. Around the edges we see the external situation he came into, his 'wonderful humility, astonishing poverty',[12] while in the convex surface of the mirror we see what could be called Christ's work, what he did during his life and how he did it. Finally, we gaze into the centre of the mirror, where we see the mystery of love and pain which we call the Cross.

She then writes a beautifully constructed passage, leading us from attending through considering to contemplating, and so on to hearing Christ's own voice from the Cross, leading us back through consideration to attention.[13] This circular movement reflects the shifting patterns of prayer in our lives, for no one can live entirely in high contemplation. We must all return to the Scriptures, to read, consider and ponder, not just once but continually until we die.

However, there is yet another aspect to this Mirror, another way of understanding the whole image, and that is as a mirror into which we look, not to see Christ, but to see ourselves. Clare applied this to life in a very practical sort of way, almost briskly: look in this Mirror, she says, and see what to put on. Look in this mirror and see what you need, see what is lacking to your humanity. Look at this prototype and see what is missing in yourself. 'Look into this mirror every day, and continually ponder on your own face, so that you may adorn your whole being, within and without, in robes of wonderful variety.'[14] So now, having shown us how to become like Christ, she begins to teach us how to articulate the differences. We need to know where we are not Christ-like, just as we need to know how to become more Christ-like. In an engaging development of the image, she tells us that if we study our face in this mirror, then we will be able to adorn our 'whole being with virtues like flowers,' that is, not only with the essentials but also with the decorative and non-functional, with that small bit extra over and beyond the obligatory, as well as 'with garments every bit as ornate as those of the daughter and beloved bride of the Most High King, for this is only fitting'. She may have in mind here the psalm about the beauty of the King's daughter being within, and perhaps she is also picking up on St Paul's image of charity as a coat which we put on over all the other guises and disguises that we wear.

She then goes on to talk about what else we will see reflected in this mirror. We will see poverty, humility and love as they are demonstrated for us in the life of Christ. She talks as if when we look into the mirror, we see both Christ and ourselves, paradigm and paradox of glory; we see what we are called to be and we see what we are. When we look into an ordinary mirror, we do so in order to see what needs to be done before we are ready to face the world and the task ahead. We look into the mirror of Christ for exactly the same reason. Clare is reminding us that when we look at ourselves in this Mirror, as in any mirror, we see a work of God, someone adorned by grace; we see the face of one loved, redeemed and made beautiful by God as well as someone in whom this work is not yet completed. These things are all quite hard to believe of ourselves, but Clare tells us that we are to be adorned with refreshment, fragrance and gentle light, the very qualities she had attributed to grace in the previous passage. She reminds us that we are not only talking about the pragmatic and the functional, but about beauty and adornment. For us, like Esther, the task to which we are called requires adornment and beauty, remembering that beauty is a test of truth.

In terms of prayer, this adornment primarily requires that we learn to be present to God, wholly there where we are physically. In the end, all beauty is God's and we reflect it when we rest in that presence. Prayer is the gift of God's goodness, so it is obvious that the first requirement is that we be there to receive it—in the widest possible meaning of 'being there'. Because we are so fractured and divided within ourselves, there is a sense in which much of our struggle with prayer consists precisely in this attempt to be present. It is a shared struggle, though; we work, as Augustine said, but God so works in us that we can work. So we might define prayer as the presence of God awaiting our presence. God is always there and when we, too, are present, communication flows as naturally as the sun shines. The life-changing element is that we are drawn out of our disintegration and into focus, and enabled, at last, to speak to the one who speaks to us.

Much is said and written today about the art of being present, about single-mindedness or one-pointedness, and in Francis and Clare we see two people who were highly skilled at it. This is part of the secret of their attractiveness and their simplicity. Put into a more modern terminology, Clare seems to have considered that, more than anything else, we are people in relationship, and the paradigm of all our relating is the way in which God relates to us. Through the quiet gazing at Christ which she recommends, we are brought into relationship with God, the original pattern of things. In consequence, all our other relationships become free to realise more of their hidden potential. We tend to see ourselves only as we are now, but God never loses sight of what we are becoming. As the *Cloud* says, God's merciful eyes look not at what we are, nor at what we have been but at what we would be. Surely the basis of all our hope is this belief God has in our future, that is, the shared future of God and humanity, and this God-based hope enables us, in our turn, to have faith in that future.

Flowing from these insights, Francis and Clare saw three modes in our relating to God. We turn to God: conversion; we undergo change: contrition; we are one with God: communion. Francis and Clare did not see these three modes as successive lessons, but saw all three present all the time in us. As always, their main concern was how to live, not how to pray, which is why they gave so little advice on the matter. In addition, Francis always stressed that while our prayer can help our life, still more the way we live can help or extinguish our prayer. Conversion, contrition and communion are a life's programme, not an extra to be fitted in now and then, and Francis used to say that he wanted the friars to 'pray unceas-

ingly with a heart free from self-interest'.[15] Our task is to make
our hearts as free from self-interest as we can. We have choices
here, and infinite scope for self-deception. We do not pray in
order to be heard or answered or to have an experience, but in
order to meet God and be available. Fortunately, God's presence to us is not measured by our awareness of it, and it is
important that we do not confuse our transient perceptions of
reality (God is absent) with reality itself (God is present). The
validity of our prayer, like the reality of God's presence, is not
tested by how we felt during prayer, but by how we acted after
it.

Seeking God, Francis maintained, was the same as seeking
joy; but the truth is that we would often prefer to be left in
peace in our pessimism, for joy demands greatness of us. He
used to say that if we, the servants of God, would strive to
have and to keep inner and outer joy, the fruit of a pure heart,
then the demons would have no power to harm us.[16] He was
also well aware of the upwardly mobile tendencies of human
nature and of how damaging this is to prayer, and he told
his brethren, time and again, never to lose touch with the
simplicity, humility and poverty with which they had begun,
because these accurately reflect the truth of our impoverished
reality.

During his lifetime, Francis tried hard to practise what he
preached, and he used to tell the others to imitate him as he
imitated Christ. There are some delightful stories about
Brother John who did this literally, sneezing when Francis
sneezed, turning round when Francis turned around. As time
went on, however, Francis' holiness led him into very great joy
while his brethren expected a more saintly gloom from him.
He asked on one occasion for a lute to accompany his singing
and the brother pretended he could not find one, as he
thought the neighbours would be shocked. There is another
story that Francis asked for wine and the brother had the
cheek to tell him that he should be content with water, out of a
spirit of poverty and in solidarity with the poor. Francis gently
acquiesced. The story goes on that when the water was
brought, it was found that the Lord had repeated the miracle
of Cana for his servant. Another time, when Francis was
seriously ill, he had the brothers singing his Praises of the
Lord day and night. In the end, Brother Elias

became concerned with St Francis' manner of comforting and cheering himself and rejoicing in the Lord when he was in such an advanced state of illness. One day he had a talk with him and said: My dear brother, for me it is a great consolation and source of edification to find you showing yourself so happy for your own and your companions' sake. On the other hand, the people of this city, who indeed deem you, living or dead, a saint, are convinced that you are gravely and incurably ill and are going to die very soon. When they hear you singing your *Canticle* so happily, they could wonder about it and start talking. They could remark to one another: That man is about to die—how is this that he can make such a show of gaiety? He ought to be thinking about death . . . Francis replied: by the grace of God and the help of the Holy Spirit, I am so closely united and at one with my Lord that by his mercy I have good reason to rejoice in Him, the All-Highest.[17]

He tells us himself that he came to this joy through meditating 'on examples left by the Son of God'.[18] This was the firm basis of all his prayer. By degrees he came to see that there is no distinction between sacred and secular, and almost none between this world and the next. Life is a whole because God is a whole. Everything is God's gift to us and in spite of all we have done to make it otherwise, the essential goodness of this gift is unharmed. We can find our way back to this essential goodness by gazing into the mirror of Christ, this clarifying crystal backed with our humanity. Jesus Christ, the embodied Word, means that there is nothing in human life, present or to come, outside the divine involvement and communion. Nothing now is profane. Nothing now is beyond the scope of God's concern. Prayer and daily living are not two entirely separate things, but through prayer we can learn to live, as Clare did, like one who embodies John's saying: The Word was the true light' (John 1:9).

When Clare and Francis first set out to imitate Christ, they did so with as great a simplicity and literalness as Brother John imitating Francis. This is probably why Francis was so patient with Brother John even though the others were driven to distraction by him. Do what Christ did, is always Clare's advice too. Love him totally, she says somewhere else, who gave himself totally for your love. Keep nothing of yourself for yourself, said Francis. This apparently unproductive squandering of resources is the heart of love, it is true self-giving with no interest in the return. Christ never said: If I love you then you must love me; but rather, The Father has loved me and I love you, and you love one another.

PART 2

Contrition

The Penances we Choose

In this chapter I would like to think a little about penance, not least because, to many people, it can seem a somewhat masochistic custom, rooted in a set of attitudes which the more enlightened among us no longer hold, something which 'went out with the Council and not before time'. It is easy, and to a certain extent correct, to feel that some periods of history, for example, the Middle Ages, were locked into a love-hate relationship with the material and physical, and that many of the extreme forms of penance then in vogue manifested this. At the time of Clare, many new models of women's religious life were springing up, characterised, among other things, by extreme fasting, and the story is told of Clare (as of others) that when she was young she fasted so severely that her health was endangered, almost ruined in fact. Today we would ask whether some of these women were not anorexic, and perhaps they did have a kind of holy anorexia, although it would seem to have been more rooted in their cultural assumptions and convictions than in the attitudes now associated with anorexia. Yet confusion about the body, and still more about sexuality, is as common today as in Clare's time, perhaps even more so, for a reading of Clare's letters gives the impression of a woman who had thoroughly probed and come to terms with her own sexuality, with her physical self and with her humanity.

Reading Clare's letters, we quickly begin to suspect that here is a spiritual guide of some stature, an articulate person speaking out of her own rare experience. Before we can come to the heart of what she has to say, however, there is a small difficulty to tidy up, and that is the 'spousal' language she uses. The main point of the problem is that 'spouse' is not a word much in use today, apart from jokes and a few forms of the Inland Revenue. Clare, without doubt, is speaking of something relevant but how can we get behind the language to the meaning? On the whole, if we translate *sponsa* by 'beloved', or even 'darling', perhaps, rather than by 'spouse', it makes better sense for our purposes: 'Look in that mirror every day, darling of Jesus Christ . . .'; or, 'You have held fast to the footprints of the one whose beloved you deservedly are.' Then we may find Clare speaking much more directly to us, about something we all long for and are eager to know, something which concerns us nearly, namely God's love for us.

It could seem that we have a gender problem here, that it might conceivably be all very well for women like Clare to see themselves as brides and darlings in relation to God, but what are men supposed to do? However, God is beyond either male or female and each pronoun is as mistaken as the other. It is our habits of thought which dictate such language, not any aspects of God. God has no gender, even while somehow being the source of the paradigms of gender. It is possible that these stand in relation to us rather as the most profound archetypes, archetypes of archetypes, perhaps; but we make a big mistake if we see God as so narrowly male that only women can appropriately enter into a unitive relationship with 'him', or if we see God as so narrow that our sexual orientation essentially governs the relationship. To some extent, it may govern the way we ourselves relate to God, because our loving is inseparable from our sexuality, but while men and women might, conceivably, deal differently with God, is there any hard evidence that God deals differently with men than women— apart (if possible) from the fact that no two people relate or pray in the same way? The important thing is that the more we interact with God, the more we are led to transcend our limitations, including the one of being primarily male or female, and the more we are drawn to enter into the infinite capacities of God. Because this works itself out on every level, our holiness will, in consequence, involve psychological and emotional maturing, as well as spiritual development.

In the mind of Francis and Clare, union with God is ours from the very start, the original given, not the goal of a long initiation. It is by experiencing God's love that we learn about love, what it is and how to do it, and so our inner boundaries continually expand. The language of the mystics is often disconcertingly erotic, partly because their inner boundaries have shifted more than ours have, and partly because this is simply all they can do, it is the best language available. Prayer, however, is not a secret, slightly devious route to sexual fulfilment, but rather, it offers a perspective so radically different from any other that all our deepest relational gifts are drawn into the realignment. While sexual expression can be a substitute for, or a barrier against, relationships, yet for many people, it is precisely sexuality which brings them back, again and again, to struggle with their relationships, however painfully. Through prayer, our sexuality and our relationships are both refocused, we become less driven and hounded by them, because our deeper needs are being met by the only one who is greater than our hunger. The relevance of all this to our attempts at penance and contrition lies in the Freudian awareness that we need to have a pleasure principle of some sort in view, and penance is no exception. To be penitential is not a sane ambition on its own; union with God is the goal of the endeavour, and we need to have this clearly in mind before we can maintain a course of any self-discipline.

Another thing which makes penance a problem for us today, is that our theology is in the process of development, so we do not have a fixed, unquestioned framework within which to site ourselves as penitents. We are not at ease with the tidy label of 'sinner', when we do our best (on the whole); we are not at ease with offering things up in union with the Passion of Christ, because it seems arrogantly to imply that Christ had not done things thoroughly; neither, on the other hand, are we at ease with the idea that all is well and we need not bother. For most of us, there is a re-education needed here, which will take place as we proceed. Certainly this was so for Francis and Clare, who were both quite punitive towards themselves at the beginning, and both had to learn balance, moderation, compassion, and self-love in its best sense.

In every skill, there are exercises done behind the scenes, which appear to bear little relationship to the actual art but which every practitioner will insist are valuable and even essential. These exercises are often traditional, deliberately chosen and practised, and one of their more important products is the honing of commitment effected through the unglamorous self-discipline of sticking to them. This was what Francis and Clare had to learn. At first, their back-stage exercises were the traditional ones of fasting, cutting back on sleep, self-denial and cultivated discomfort. The art in which they grew so skilled was human living at its most free and loving. Their later back-stage exercises were their steadfast adherence to joy, gentleness, patience, tenderness. In her first fervour, when she still had much to learn, Clare kept vigil for so much of the night and abstained from food to such an extent, that her sisters became greatly alarmed. They begged her with tears not to be so rash or stubborn, and in the event they were proved right because she became ill. Even so, it took the combined commands of Francis and the Bishop to persuade her to eat daily. Asked how she knew this, the witness at the Canonisation Process replied tersely that she had lived with her.

This offers us the first guideline, that if we set out to do penance, we must never lose sight of *whose* penance it is supposed to be. Francis, as it happened, was no less extreme than Clare in this matter, though he did advise the friars not to give the body grounds for complaint. Only in this, says his biographer, did his actions differ from his words[1] and, in fact, towards the end of his life Francis apologised to his Brother Body, who had supported him so faithfully and for so long, receiving in return such rough treatment.

Celano also makes the important point that the early friars, who lived lives of quite rash penance and austerity, had to learn to base it on constancy, and on this foundation they then built a structure of love.[2] These men were remarkably like us in their blend of good intentions and bad performance, and they continually swung from one extreme to the other: 'If, as can happen, their sobriety was disturbed by an abundance of food and drink . . . they mortified themselves very sharply by an abstinence of many days.'[3] Undoubtedly they would have done better with a little less of both! While it is important to fast and do penance, it is more important not to use it as disguised self-punishment. It is most important of all to know when to relax, because the ability to celebrate is the hallmark of authentic spirituality. Once one of Francis' brothers woke up crying with the pain of hunger, certain that he was dying. Francis not only made him a meal but also woke the others up to join in. He then told them that to over-fast was as bad as to over-eat. Every sacrifice, he said, must be seasoned with salt. Celano goes on to tell us that these brothers were still very new in the spiritual life and therefore prone to excessive penances[4]—in other words, they had it all to learn.

Clare gave similar advice to Agnes of Prague, telling her to refrain from an impossible and indiscreet austerity, saying: '[so act] that living, you may praise the Lord, giving to him your reasonable service, and let your sacrifice always be seasoned with salt.'[5] This seasoning with salt that they both mention is in accordance with the instruction in Leviticus about sacrifice (Lev. 2:13), and they understood it to represent that sense of proportion and that pinch of dry humour which stop us taking things too seriously. Our human nature will be slightly comic no matter what we do, and there is much wisdom in peacefully enjoying it, so we can season our serious approach to spirituality with a touch of astringency.

Although most of us probably feel that excessive penances are less of a problem to us than lack of penance, yet many people feel a real need for more self-discipline in their lives and are puzzled as to how they should set about it. We know well that it can be almost impossible to break habits of over-indulgence without a certain pendulum swing, and we should not despise this method. The extremes of our folly can become the boundaries of our hunger for God, so it is good and helpful to fast, to be uncomplainingly cold or hot or uncomfortable, to cut back on sleep and, above all, not to talk about these things. Sooner or later common sense asserts itself and we become more aware of the bad temper which follows fasting and sleeplessness, and the subtle pride which accompanies them. The story was told by Hubert Van Zeller OSB, of a certain man who once said to himself: I am probably the only man on Reading station in a hair shirt, and realised that he should take it off as soon as possible! Such moments of truth will come to us all. Like the 'certain man', we must avoid falling into one weakness (smugness) while we are escaping another (the unspecified reason for the hair shirt).

We may also come to realise that our thrust towards penance is partly rooted in self-hatred or hatred of our humanity. Most of us have negative hang-ups of one sort or another, and as we move more seriously into our life of prayer, they will tend to be thrown to the surface. It will help if we realise that this is a good sign, not a cause for anxiety, because it indicates that our prayer is seeping down to the layers which need healing and redemption. So we are not more neurotic because we have begun to pray, but we may appear to be, because when we start praying regularly, our negative attitudes, which were previously cemented over, begin to push to the surface. To some extent, this never ends; it is almost as if we are constantly in the process of being created, so that there is always more of us to be brought to God. Even in the last two years of his life, after he had received the stigmata, Celano tells us that Francis still did not consider that he had laid hold of his goal, but was still hoping to make a start.[6] Even on his death-bed, he was saying: 'Let us now begin to serve God because up to now we have done nothing.'

One caution on penance, which some must take into account, is that strand in the Celtic temperament, and possibly others too, which lays it open to extremism in a particular way and which is really a life-denying kind of puritanism: if I enjoy it, it must be bad, or bad for me, or both. In addition to this, too much fasting and too little sleep affect our chemical balance and with it our judgement, so it can seem to us that with a little less food and a little less sleep, we will come to know the answer to the riddle of the world, like Odin hanging for nine days on the tree Yg-Drasil. This is a great illusion. Most of these imbalances and aberrations arise because we look more at ourselves than at God, and have forgotten Clare's good advice, that whatever we do should give praise to God. This, the touchstone of authentic penance, will gradually establish itself, but it cannot possibly do so unless we are, to some extent, doing penance. Dieting, too—however penitential—must not be confused with penance, though it can have a place in our practices of penance if our weight is a symptom of tolerated inner disorder and our dieting is part of our commitment to rectifying that.

To begin to do penance, however, is to begin to discover our absolute need for grace and help from God. Not all our motives are suspect and many of the maturer reasons for penance will be present right from the start of our prayer life. It is the egocentric ones that we will blush about later, and many of them can be flushed out by two simple questions. The first is: Do we tell our friends? The second is: Do we tell our director or the equivalent? We are not doing penance for the sake of the kudos (or the disapproval) among our unconverted friends and relations. A situation can easily arise in which they know all about our day of fasting or our night of prayer, and yet we are reluctant to submit these self-imposed disciplines to the judgement of the one who stands as a reference-point to us. We need to reflect on this reluctance. Left to ourselves, we tend to take on too much and maintain too little, and a good director will help us find a realistic point of balance. 'Our flesh is not bronze nor is our strength that of stone. We are fragile and prone to every kind of weakness of body, and so, my dearest, I pray and beg you in the Lord to have the wisdom and prudence to hold back from any extreme or impossible austerity',[7] says Clare to Agnes of Prague, to whom Clare stood, in some measure, as a guide. This was good advice, given to someone whose commitment was undoubted but whose experience was still limited. A good director can be counted on to point out any absence of wisdom or prudence, as well as to challenge our motives, whether they express themselves in too much or too little penance.

The single, most powerful, motive for penance is the growing importance of God in our lives, together with the fact that it is difficult to pray when we are undisciplined or manipulative or cutting corners on integrity. We soon find that either the relationship with God or the corner-cutting must go, and if we try to maintain them both, for example, prayer and dishonesty in business, we will run into real trouble. Usually we can see this for ourselves, but we are so skilled at self-deception that it will help us to have someone with whom we can check out the counterweights we are putting against our tendency to sin.

This person should be a sounding-board, not a map-maker, for Christ (the Way) is our map and the Spirit is our guide. A director should know our story in its broad outlines and listen on a regular basis to what we have to say about our life with God. He or she should not be too fond of us to challenge us, but should have enough native empathy to enable us to talk openly. At the very least, a director should help us to distinguish difficulties of our own making from God's invitation to take a further step forward.

Another extremely important aspect of penance, fasting and generally cutting back, is the implicit solidarity with those who have less than we do. Francis said once: It makes me very ashamed when I find a man who is poorer than myself.[8] Admittedly he had taken a vow to have nothing of his own, but he speaks for us all in some measure. Through fasting, we commit ourselves to co-operate with Christ as he works to make the world the way it was meant to be, because we assist in this process, even by the smallest and simplest restoration of a balance due in justice. There is still enough food for everyone if we would only cut back and share; our fasting is nothing compared with the permanent malnourishment of more than half the world. Both Francis and Clare, who saw that everything on the earth is God's gift, given equally to each of us, considered that they were stealing if they had more than they needed while others did not have enough. This is what Francis meant by saying that he felt indicted when he met someone who had less than he. The message of this attitude in the light of today's injustices, needs no spelling out.

Generally speaking, the disciplines of penance help us to stay heading in the right direction, focused on this elusive concept of wholeness. They are a way of keeping our eyes where we wish them to be. If we follow our whims, we will lose any steadfastness, for it is not native to us to be faithful, as Francis and Clare well knew. Steadfastness comes with grace and with desire, that is, if we want it, we will be given it. The struggle which we experience when we begin to do penance is because change and instability have such a strong hold on us that to wrench ourselves free is almost like dying. In some respects this does get easier as we go along, because we gradually come to share in the stability and steadfastness of God. In every religious ascesis, there is a stripping process of self-discipline, by which we seek to free ourselves in order to give ourselves, in order to be at the disposal of God and our neighbours. The early friars saw clearly that they must give themselves to help others in their need,[9] and self-sacrifice, springing from our desire to love, is one way of learning these skills of self-giving.

In all this, Christ is our blueprint. Like Clare, the brothers found that the more they gazed at 'the poor, condemned Christ', the more their values and thought patterns were changed. When we ourselves redress imbalances, we tend to do so by adding the opposite, in the hope that things will cancel each other out. Christ redresses our imbalances by lifting them up on to another plane and showing us that they are complementary. God's view, the transcendent view, is always unitive, and it reveals to us that opposites are mutually necessary, that they unite in Christ to form a whole, like a sphere. We tend to deny what we do not like or cannot handle, our weaknesses, for instance, or our sins; but Christ actually moved right into them, he 'became sin for us'. By doing so, he transformed both sin and suffering, as well as the death which is their term, and still he arose alive from the grave. By being chosen from within in this way, both material and moral emptiness were, and can still be, radically altered and redirected. 'He wanted to appear in the world as a man who was despised, in need and poor so that people might become rich in him by possessing the kingdom of heaven—for they were extremely poor and needy, starved by this great lack of heavenly nourishment.'[10]

So Francis and Clare recommended penance for everybody, seeing it as externalised co-operation with grace. By it, we strengthen ourselves, so that we do not continue to collapse at the first sign of temptation. On the other hand, we also learn our need for grace through it, that we are not our own redeemers. We often tend to want all the credit for ourselves and to settle our own destiny. Francis says that as soon as we make our will 'mine' instead of God's, we 'exalt ourselves over the good things which the Lord is saying and doing' in us. This, in his view, is what the 'original' sin was. We find it hard to live with the insecurity of grace, we want salvation to be securely ours, rather than God's gift of glory. Understanding this, Francis advises us: 'Try to realise the dignity God has conferred on you. He created and formed your body in the image of his beloved Son and your soul in his own likeness.'[11]

Inspired by these insights of Francis and Clare, Franciscan thinkers have gone on to maintain that even had there been no need for redemption, Christ would still have become man because he is the focus of God's creative activity. As that honorary Franciscan, the Jesuit Teilhard de Chardin, saw so clearly, Christ is the glorious sum and summit of creation. The incarnation was not a divine contingency plan because things had gone wrong. In Genesis, God said: Man has become one of us; and Francis and Clare saw that God has become one of *us*. The coming of the Word in flesh means that there is now nothing in human life which is outside the divine involvement. Nothing is profane, nothing is secular or godless, but even in the farthest reaches of life, apparently the most distant from God, we find hidden the Christ who became sin for us. There are no separate compartments for holiness and badness, but only the redemptive and creative presence of God, always at work in all that is, yeast in our dough.

This was a life-changing realisation for Francis, as it is for us, and it was here that he found his most serious motives for living differently. At first he simply acted against what he had been, disciplining his body because he knew only too well how it became a tyrant if he did not, refusing to have anything to do with money because, as Assisi's golden boy, he was aware of the way money can tie us into knots of power and greed. Latterly, much of his penance took the form of concern for others, willingness to carry his own burdens and to become cheerful again—often the hardest of all. Even Francis did not always succeed. He struggled with a certain thing for two years, and then one day heard the Gospel read:

> If you had faith as a grain of mustard seed, you would tell a mountain to move from where it is and go somewhere else and that would be done. Francis replied: What is this mountain? The answer was given him: This mountain is your temptation. St Francis said: Therefore, Lord, let it be done to me as you have said. Immediately he was freed, and so completely that he was as if he had never had the temptation.[12]

One wonders what it was.

In spite of this, or, more probably, because of it, his companions tell us that his chief concern was to remain spiritually joyful, both within and without. In this way, he said, the demons had no power over him. Joy, he maintained, is our most sure defence against temptation. Francis and Clare both considered joy to be something we can choose to have, an option, not a chance, the unexpected companion of genuine penance. When a brother was gloomy one day, Francis said sternly that any sorrow he felt was to be kept between himself and God, not off-loaded on to other people. He also said: When I am in a bad humour, if I can look at my companion and see how he is filled with joy, then because of his cheerfulness I can leave the temptation and bad humour behind and get back my inner joy.[13] Much of Francis' advice is practical, like this, and very simple. He talked about ordinary, undramatic stuff: fulfilling our daily tasks, supporting others who seem weaker than we are, co-operating with grace, rejecting the habitual temptations which sneak along beside us, not allowing ourselves to be overwhelmed by gloom or bitterness or sadness but choosing to acknowledge that the Lord is always cause for rejoicing.

Clare told Agnes that we can only take hold of the treasure of the Gospel through the truth about ourselves, and the hands and arms by which we hold it are poverty of spirit and inner freedom. God, she went on, made everything from nothing and hid a treasure in the heart of it all. When we acknowledge our nothingness compared with God, then we begin to get free from what she calls 'the emptiness that makes human hearts so foolish'.[14] It is as if she were balancing emptiness against nothingness, playing around with the two concepts: the emptiness which we try to escape from, which leads us deeper and deeper into illusion; the nothingness, which, when we acknowledge it, becomes the raw material of God's work in us.

Clare, like Francis, read the drama of Eden as the personal story of each one of us, and saw the effect it has had on us, the way it has inverted our values. We wonder why the Word is so hard to read and do not realise that we are seeing things upside-down. As a result, we consider innocence to be something we once had but have now lost, rather than a condition yet to be attained. We define innocence primarily in sexual terms and see purity as equal to virginity, virginity as merely physical. In our relationship with God, we will come to learn that it is all the other way around and that chastity, purity and virginity are words about an integrity and a wholeness to which, although invited, we have not yet come. It is love itself which creates chastity, self-giving which generates purity, and abandoning ourselves which brings us to integrity. We are talking here about experience, not about understanding. We are also talking about a woman's thoughts on love and celibacy. Innocence and the Garden of Eden are the goal of all our travelling and Clare tells us how we shall arrive there:

When you have loved him, you will be chaste,
when you have touched him, you will be pure,
when you have taken him to yourself, you will then be a
    virgin.[15]

On the whole, Clare lived through an experience and understood it afterwards, and we, like her, learn experientially that God is our way to wholeness simply because we discover that we become more integrated as we grow nearer to God. This is a simple fact of experience. When we are in God's presence, we are drawn towards the oneness of the Godhead, which is virginity in its deepest and even in its mystical sense. In the Christmas liturgy,[16] St Hypolitus declares that since Christ has become man, we now share the Godhead and have become divine, and he goes on to talk about this divinity in a way which leaves no doubt about his literal understanding of the phrase (although he also makes it clear that he does not confuse us in any way with God). Hypolitus is saying the same as the prayer during the Mass, that as Christ shared our human nature, so may we be brought to share in his divine nature. We might even suggest that the original lost virginity is the rift between God and ourselves, the destruction of an integrated creation.

Francis, who came to a very visible and complete sharing in the life of Christ, always spoke of his beginning in prayer as: when I began to do penance. In one of his talks to his brothers, Francis draws a picture of this life of prayer and penance, adding quality after quality, describing it as a life in which we show compassion for our neighbour, do not think differently of ourselves when praised than when blamed (or vice versa), when we weigh what we should say and how we should reply, when we quietly agree with a rebuke and make no excuses for ourselves, when we are as humble with those under us as with those over us, when we love someone as much when sick as when well, when absent as when present. He used to say that we cannot know ourselves while everything is going well, 'but when those who should co-operate do the exact opposite, then we can tell. A man has as much patience and humility as he has then, and no more;'[17] and later on he added: What a man is before God, that he is and no more.[18]

The Pain we do not Seek

Francis knew well that however much our life is lived in God and however much we choose to live in joy, there are still times when sorrow chooses us. These are times when grief or pain brutally invade our lives, and we, the clay pot, are plunged into fires which subject us to so much strain that the clay itself cracks. As in most processes, to be done to is much more painful than to choose to do, and so far, we have mainly considered those penances and self-disciplines which we choose for ourselves. As we have seen, these have an important role in our spiritual life and are a necessary part of accepting responsibility for our lives and our choices. However, the most demanding struggles, and the ones which most mature us, psychologically and spiritually, are those that come upon us unsought, always undesired and for which we feel we have had no preparation at all. The struggles that we freely undertake, such as fasting, are much easier, simply because we remain in control. We can always decide to stop. What, though, are we to make of those formative experiences of pain and distress which we do not choose and do not like, perhaps can hardly bear, and which we cannot bring to an end when we are tired of them? What of those situations of trauma that we have to survive somehow, and which can drag us so low that survival is all we look for (and such situations come to many people in one form or another)? What becomes of joy then? What happens then to our prayer and our praise and our thanksgiving? Are they possible in such a situation? Is it even right, in pain and loss and trauma, to try to give thanks? What are the characteristics of this time when such things happen to us?

Almost everybody has at least one period of disintegration and disruption in their lives and it is a time of immense importance in our prayer journey simply because it is so difficult. We may be talking about an illness, a bereavement, prolonged physical pain, a breakdown or an attack of one sort or another, but every time, the primary characteristic of the experience is that it is imposed upon us, we do not choose it and would give a great deal, possibly everything, to avoid it. By that fact alone we feel robbed of our freedom, even plunged into the position of being victimised, at another's mercy, exploited. Sometimes we can see it coming, as when we know that sick person will soon die, but even that does not prepare us for what happens to us when they do die. There is no preparation for this, which is why it is so searching, and when it comes we have no resources except the naked truth of ourselves. It is quite literally an *angustia* a narrow place, in which we are straitened. I am in dire straits, we say, speaking the truth.

In the midst of illness, bereavement, trauma, pain or breakdown, we live differently, as if pared to the bone in some way. So many of the things about which we were formerly busy, now lie undone, and we find that it does not seem to matter much. With the passage of time many of these things may leach back into our lives, but never with quite the same demanding hold over us because we cannot obliterate (though we may deny) the time when they lay undone and it did not matter. Such a period of disruption, in which so many things are relativised, leaves us radically altered, so that even if we move back into an external life which is apparently the same, we will have been changed within it. The touch of something absolute will have seared and metamorphosed us as heat changes the rocks of the earth so that, like the planet itself, the bedrock of ourselves is altered. Through it all, God works in our being, as we grapple with cosmic forces in the context of our small lives. On a deeper level than ever before, we become Golgotha and the Garden, where death and resurrection wrestle. Death and disease and destruction are revealed as intrinsic to the fabric of our existence, part of the cosmic dislocation with which we struggle. No wonder that we are shaken to the core.

It is typical of this experience that we cannot prepare ourselves for it. While, like Job, we make no claim to be sinless, like Job we still fail to see any parity between what has happened to us and what we have done, and a spirituality which sees our relationship with God solely in terms of reward and punishment is revealed as inadequate. People ask: What have I done? and there is no answer because, in the last analysis, this is the wrong question. We are not obliged to argue ourselves into the conviction that this tragedy is our own fault. We may be able to connect it with the presence of sin in the world, but it may well be that the only honest answer to the question: What have I done to deserve this? is 'Nothing'. And in one form or another, we all tend to ask this question, either in bewilderment, anger, reproach or guilt.

When we look at Francis and Clare, it can seem to us today that they lived in a kind of perpetual delight, although we know that this was not how they themselves saw it, and we may legitimately ask: how did they manage when winter came to their spirit? No human story would be quite normal if it had no share in pain—and what became of their spirituality then, what became of their serenity and joy? In this searching test, what happened to them? Did their prayer and joy, bought at a high price, sink without a trace?

Did Francis and Clare know any such experiences? For example, to take the trauma of bereavement, what happened to Clare when Francis died? She was only thirty-three or four when this happened, so how did she cope? Did she cope? She herself, years later, told us only one thing about this time. In addition, although we have no extant letters from this period, there are two other sources of information. One is the *Legend of Perugia*, almost certainly written by Brother Leo, one of Francis' first companions. The second in Celano's *First Life*, written soon after Francis' death when Clare was still alive and in her prime, when all the brethren who had lived through that event were also alive, ready to correct and be critical if Celano's account strayed from their memories of what had happened. Leo tells us that during the week before Francis died, when Clare herself was gravely ill,

> Lady Clare . . . wept bitterly and could not console herself at the thought of not seeing him again before his death, her only father next to God, her interior and external comfort, he who was the first one to establish her solidly in the grace of the Lord, She made this known to him through the intermediary of a brother.[1]

There were several occasions when Clare 'made this known to him through the intermediary of a brother' and we get the impression of a very easy rapport and mutual understanding between them all. Just as the brethren watched over Francis with love and awe, so they seem to have watched over the relationship between Francis and Clare with great concern and support. Her grief grieved them. Nearly all Italian, their emotional responses were instant and warm, and while they did not doubt it, they also never ceased to be amazed at the transcendent chastity of this relationship. They well knew what Francis' death would mean to Clare and did not think it chance that when he was dying, she also became gravely ill.

Francis was for Clare something of what Isaac had been for Abraham—the life-changing gift of God, the mark of God's love and the focus of response to God. It seems that for most of us there is an Isaac or a Francis, something or someone without whom we cannot imagine how to live—or cannot, before the loss, conceive how we could live after it. Often this person in some way expresses the handful of values without which our life would have no meaning for us. This Isaac is a human factor mediating the transcendent to us; a focus of good in our lives, even the Good in our life. To lose such an Isaac can be an experience so searing that it forms a plimsoll line against which we measure and date events. 'This was not as terrible as when . . .' or 'That happened before . . .' we say. Kierkegaard, in his imaginative reflections on Abraham, suggests that Abraham never forgot and never recovered from this act that God had so nearly asked of him. He was so scorched by the experience, Kierkegaard suggests, that he could never laugh again. Since the name Isaac means Laughter, this is to say that in a certain sense Isaac did indeed die on the mountain. Such a reflection and such an experience move us, instantly and mercilessly, into the heart of the incomprehensible. Like Abraham, we may never be able to forget how dreadful it was or what it cost. We may never be the same after it, because to have done something impossible means that we had, first, to become different people from what we were before. Thus Abraham was more changed than Isaac. On that mountain, even though Isaac was spared, Abraham died in a certain sense. Death is not always where we think it is; the one who lives on can feel the more dead. Yet the people had a saying, relates the author of Genesis, that on the mountain God will provide.

All of this was true for Clare too. So much grace had come

to her through Francis. Faced with the prospect of him dying, and being at that time very ill herself, she 'wept bitterly and could not console herself at the thought of not seeing him again before his death', and as events turned out, she did not. Even the saints cannot mould events to their wishes, so our failure to do so must not dismay us. We are part of something bigger, and events take their course, driven by some other logic than our desires. Strong-minded as she was, Clare 'could not console herself'—she tried and failed. Many years later she was to write that she remembered 'the frailty, which frightened me in myself, after the death of our holy Father Francis; he was our pillar of strength and, apart from God, our only consolation and support.'[2] Her Latin implies that she had feared finding herself so frail, had found herself so, and had found it frightening to be so. It seems as if a pit of weakness in herself was revealed to her. Until then, she had always been stronger than any challenge that life could throw at her. She had ridden on a crest of love and enthusiasm and success. Now, perhaps for the first time, she saw possibilities of such frailty in herself that years later she still remembered it with dread.

Surely the 'frailty I had feared' was the real possibility that she would not find the strength to cope with the loss of Francis, himself her 'pillar of strength'—precisely what she had lost. Without him, she could not confront the loss of him. For Clare too, it was not just a matter of comfort but of resources. The only hope of comfort or resource lay in seeing the living Francis again, the very thing which was denied her. She had no private moments for farewell, no opportunity to draw together the threads of their world-changing relationship, no chance for gratitude and advice and tenderness. She was left, to be turned alone on the lathe of time, for there was still living wood to be shaped in her. Like us, she tasted the bitter mystery of unanswered prayer. Perhaps she realised what we ignore: that the wish for every prayer to be answered is a recipe for chaos. Perhaps she remembered what we forget: that No with God is as creative as Yes. Perhaps she neither realised nor remembered, but merely endured, which is what we do too.

When Francis finally died, the friars brought his dead body to San Damiano so that Clare and her sisters could see him for the last time. This was her only chance to say goodbye to him.

It was also another opportunity to do what the friars had been doing—gaze with amazement at the wounds in his hands, feet and side, the stigmata. Until then, the friars had been caught up on a crest of exultation as they saw, many of them for the first time, 'in the middle of his hands and feet, not indeed the holes made by the nails but the nails themselves formed out of his flesh and retaining the blackness of iron, and his right side was red with blood'.[3] In a triumphant procession, with a great crowd of people singing and with the band playing, the people of Assisi set out to take their saint home. On the way they stopped at San Damiano and, placing the coffin so that the sisters could see it, opened it.

At that moment, the whole tone of the account changes and the glory and the singing, the exultation, the festivity and the band, are all silenced before grief. We are moved, in a few sentences, from the triumph of having a local saint, to a deep and terrible personal loss and Celano puts on Clare's lips a kind of lament in which she sees undreamed-of vistas of emptiness opening before her. He was all I had, she cries.

We see her, during this lament, move through all the stages of grief. She is incredulous: 'What shall we do? Are you forsaking us now in our misery? In whose care are you going to leave us in our desolation?' The impossible had happened, something quite different from the way she had always thought it would be. Although she was so much younger than Francis, her health was so bad that it had not been unrealistic of her to think that she might die first, she had 'wanted to die first in order to welcome you on the other side'. It is also possible that her imagination had fixed on this because the alternative scenario (which now confronted her) had been unthinkable. She could not believe that he would not be there.

We hear the extravagant words of her anger: 'What do you want us to do, shut up in this prison? How terrible is death! By taking you, it kills us.' Celano might have ironed these words out a little, had not so many still been alive who had witnessed the event (including Clare herself). To have her talking about being 'shut up in this prison' was hardly consonant with the image he was defining for her as a model of holiness and 'Queen of peace'. For us, now, her words enable us to look into her pain and even into her panic and they make her more credible as a person and give her greater authority as an example. Conformity with God is easy for no one, not even for

Clare, whose sisters later called her 'the footprint of the Mother of God'.[4] This was the journey which made her that footprint, for she saw strong parallels between Mary, receiving the Word of God, keeping his words in her heart, receiving his wounded body after his death; and herself, brought to Christ by Francis, listening to Francis' teaching and remaining faithful to it through all the storms which came to the Order, and—above all—receiving Francis' wounded body after his death. In a profound way, Clare shared Mary's experience, and this gave her a most tender insight into Mary's life and feelings.

We see Clare's reproach: 'What an unfriendly leave-taking! Who will comfort us? Who will strengthen us? Who will console us?' We also see her 'torn between sorrow and joy', answering herself as she looks beyond her own pain to the wonders God had done in Francis and taking comfort from that: the sisters kissed his hands and feet and saw them wounded.

Finally we see the beginnings of resignation: when he had finally been taken away 'the door was closed to them which will hardly be opened again for such great sorrow. Hardly anyone could refrain from weeping when the angels of peace wept so bitterly.'[5] There is almost a note of relief in the account when we reach the moment when the door is closed. The friars, a little sheepishly, were glad to leave such distress, to close the door and go away. Clare was left alone to cope as best she could, because in the end, no one else can do our grieving for us. Grief is a solitary pilgrimage.

Clare now experienced the loss of no longer being known. Francis knew Clare's story, he knew all that was in her heart and to a unique degree, he knew her. With the loss of this, followed the feeling that there was no one to talk to. 'All our consolation departs with you. No solace like it remains to us.' In some radical way, she was silenced, as we are always silenced and estranged by trauma, feeling our way among customs with which everyone else seems familiar and only we at a loss. Our everyday land has become a strange country through which we walk uncertainly. This death is killing me, Clare says in effect, 'O most dreadful death.'

Because bereavement throws us into new places, it has the particular effect that we meet God, too, in new places, places where we would rather not be and from which we are denied exit. We must now make our home in another world, in the barren foothills of most dreadful death. Until time finally reasserts itself, we must live by habit, and meet a God who is not a Lord of solutions but a Sharer of situations. God is in what is. Prayer is that moment when we, too, remain in what is. Prayers, more or less wild, may come and go, but our union with God is in the truth of our situation. Slowly we learn that there is peace and a kind of healing in our attempts to rest in our reality. Much later, it will become clear, to our amazement, that the threads of prayer had never even frayed.

Is this what Clare did during that period of bereavement and adjustment? Do we know enough to reconstruct anything helpful about how she prayed? Indeed we do, because she tells us herself, although she words it in a figurative way and says that she willingly bound herself 'again and again to our Lady, most holy Poverty'.[6] Obviously this is a recollection in tranquility; but what she seems to be saying is that in her loss, she tried to choose what was inevitable; that having lost her 'all', she opened her heart to having nothing, to 'our Lady, most holy Poverty'. She grappled with the sense of being at the mercy of destructive events by accepting the reality of those events rather than by denial of them. It was not a battle to be won easily, she had to recommit herself to it again and again, but by acting as a free person once more, she found a way through and out of the sense of being flotsam on the tide of hostile happenings. Destruction and creation, hostility and friendliness lie, she discovered, in our hearts as well as in external events, for the external may wound us, but it can only destroy if it finds an ally within us.

This is demonstrated very clearly in Francis when he received the stigmata, the wounds of Christ. The sources make it quite clear that they were very real wounds, but because Francis himself had come to such inner integrity and simplicity, he received, indeed became, a true likeness to Christ. His path to this integrity, however, had been through the failure of his dream. It was the storms and rows within the Order which had nearly destroyed Francis, but he weathered them—and was tempered in the process—because he constantly struggled to return to his own inner vision and integrity, and to allow nothing to deflect him from living as he felt the Lord had called him to live. There is a true sense in which nothing can damage the person who has come to total inner integrity, but because most of us have not yet come to this, we are wounded, sometimes severely, by the events which happen to us.

In time of trauma we need, more than ever, to hold fast to Christ's words that the truth will set us free. It is nonsense to try and persuade ourselves it was God's will that we should have been raped or mugged or bereaved or suddenly made homeless. These things happened because there is sin in the world, and why there is sin in the world is a mystery even Christianity does not wholly explain, but the great insight which Christianity does contribute is surely St Paul's assertion that all things work together for good for those who love God, even sin. At such a time, truth alone can be our prayer. Our most honest feelings, no matter how negative, are all we can truthfully bring to God. We maintain ourselves in pain if we refuse to acknowledge the feelings which that pain has generated in us. When Christ said that the truth would set us free, he was not just making a philosophical statement, but he was giving us a principle for living which could guide us through any labyrinth.

Clare was saying the same thing in different words when, writing in her old age, she tells us that the way she handled these things was to open herself, willingly—that is by choice— to the very experience which was so impossible. 'We bound ourselves to our Lady Poverty.'

Brothers, Sisters and Mothers of the Lord

Francis once wrote a note full of tenderness to Brother Leo in which he said:

> My son, I want to speak to you like a mother to her child. In this one word, this single piece of advice, I want to sum up all the things that we said on our journey, and in case at any time in the future you still feel you need advice from me, I want to say to you: Whatever way you think you will most please our Lord God and will best follow in his footsteps and his poverty, do that, with the blessing of the Lord God and in obedience to me. And if you want to come to me and you need to, either for the peace of your soul or for comfort, then come, Brother Leo.[1]

Because they loved them so much, Francis and Clare were always greatly encouraging to their companions, nurturing the life of Christ in their hearts. 'And if you want to come to me and you need to, either for the peace of your soul or for comfort, then come, Brother Leo.' Clare, in 1235, wrote an equally encouraging letter to Agnes of Prague, at a time when Agnes, it seems, had begun to flag a little. In a very early edition, this letter[2] is firmly headed 'Concerning the Strong Perseverance in a Good Proposal'. In it, Clare basically says that Agnes has started out well, thanks to the grace of God, and what she must now do is keep going. She is not to be deterred by anything, either from without (where the Pope was trying to impose his own Rule on her) or from within (by discouragement or discomfort).

Clare then talks to her about struggle and single-mindedness, calling these the fruits of 'holding fast to the footprints' of Christ. She constantly reiterates that we are called to follow in the footprints of 'the poor, condemned Christ'. She does not say to Agnes, daughter of princes, that because you have

'despised the splendours of an earthly kingdom and considered the offers of an imperial marriage to be of little value',
therefore you are invited to a heavenly version of all these.
Rather, she says, you have won the Father's love by 'holding
fast to the footprints' of the poor Christ, and you have shown
this by the way you have withdrawn from temporal glories.
'Rather', we hear echoing, 'blessed is the one who hears the
word of God and keeps it' (Luke 11:28). Better to be a keeper
of the Word than even to be the Mother of the Lord. Best of all
to keep the Word and become a mother of the Lord, for
Francis and Clare both loved the insight that we are all called
to be mothers of Christ in each other. We are all called to
bring the Word to life in each other's lives. 'This is our
honour', said Clare, 'that, in our hearts (by our love) we bear
God.'

The exact nature of Christ's material poverty is, and may
always remain, a subject of controversy, certainly Franciscans
have argued about it enough, but there can be no doubt about
Christ's total self-giving. Francis and Clare saw that the one
person who really matched the self-giving of Christ was Mary,
Christ's mother, and they longed for their response to God to
be marked by that same totality as hers, and, as a consequence, by that same fruitfulness.

For Francis, the call to follow in Christ's footsteps, and live
in poverty, was an invitation to share the creative inner liberty
of Christ himself. Christ was a truly free man. When conflict
came, he could not be bought. It is clear that he was in no way
tied down or imprisoned by material possessions, nor did he
need to gather them around him, like buttresses, before he
could function. Francis began by wanting to follow Christ in
the externals of his itinerant life as a preacher, but as his love
for God grew, so his understanding of the interaction between
giving everything and being spiritually fruitful, deepened. He
sought, more and more ardently, to identify with the total self-
emptying of Christ on the cross. He also acknowledged, in
simple justice, that he had nothing which had not been given
him by God, so surely he could follow God's example and give
it away in his turn. He knew of no reason why he should
appropriate to himself more than his own portion of necessi-
ties and saw that the way to be most God-like is to give and to
share, because giving and sharing are what God does in our
regard. He took literally Peter's injunction about being sub-

ject to every human creature for God's sake (1 Pet. 2:13), and
for this reason he and his brothers went out to work for lay
people as servants and labourers, the only proviso being that
they should not be responsible for the money or the wine! He
trusted the word of Isaiah, that the Spirit of the Lord would
rest on everyone who did these things (cf. Isa. 11:2) and he
longed to be included among those whom the Lord acknowledged as his brothers and sisters and mothers (cf. Matt.
12:50).

In the first part of the Letter which he wrote to the faithful
telling them all this, Francis spells out the blessedness of
loving God with all our heart and soul, mind and strength. He
then points out that this is not the goal but only the preparation, for the task we are all called to is a sharing in God's
two-fold work of creation and redemption. The Spirit of the
Lord would rest upon the men and women who did these
things, he said.[3]

He then tells us how to set about taking our part in God's
work of creation and redemption. Steeped in Scripture as he
was, he had realised the extent to which Mary, the Mother of
the Lord, is our exemplar here. For Francis and Clare, Mary
was the paradigm of all Christian living. They learnt the craft
of discipleship from her as she summed it up in her words at
Cana: Do whatever he tells you. They learnt the value of
poverty from her as well as from Christ. 'Do not wish ever to
have anything else (than highest poverty) for the name of our
Lord Jesus Christ and his most holy Mother', said Clare to
her sisters in the Rule.[4] They saw Mary as one who demanded
nothing and offered everything, and that through her co-operation, God was able to give the world a unique revelation of
himself. As they pondered on the words in Matthew chapter
12, however, they realised that what Christ was saying goes
beyond discipleship, he was saying that everyone can be his
mother, differently but as truly as Mary. We do this by doing
what she did—the will of God. In a very striking phrase,
Francis spoke of Mary as 'the virgin made church',[5] which
sounds much more like Vatican II than the early thirteenth
century. He meant by this that Mary lived to the full what the
Church is called to live. She became the harbinger of the
Church, in the original meaning of the word: one who goes
ahead to prepare lodgings; because she became, in its fullness,
what all Christians are called to be, namely, bearers of the

Word. The Church was founded to bear Good News, Mary was the mother of the Word of that News made human.

In a certain historical sense, that motherhood could only happen once, but in another sense this bearing Christ in the world needs to be going on continually. In one way, Mary was the one mother of Christ, in another way, she was the first of many, the prototype. Through responding to God's invitation to openness and receptivity, an invitation addressed to us all, she brought forth physically the one we are invited to bring forth spiritually. Because she was open and receptive, she received God into her being so entirely that she became, in Francis' words, his robe. 'Hail, his palace!' he sang. 'Hail his home, hail his robe.'[6] In her own flesh, she clothed God's message of reconciliation, she gave a body to Christ. The wonder is that the story does not stop there: 'As the glorious virgin of virgins carried Christ materially in her body, you too, by following in his footprints, especially those of poverty and humility, can, without any doubt, always carry him spiritually.'[7]

This simple insight, far from easy to live out, became a key idea for Francis and Clare, namely that our Christian calling is to be the mothers of our Lord Jesus Christ. 'We are mothers to him' said Francis 'when we enthrone him in our hearts by love, with a pure and sincere conscience; and we give him birth by doing good, through his "holy manner of working" which should be seen by others so as to give them an example to follow.'[8] He then refers again to Matthew's Gospel: 'Let your light so shine that others may see your good works and give the glory to your Father in heaven' (Matt. 5:16).

We have already seen Clare's honest acceptance of her call to be an example to others, and her conviction that the rest of the sisters, too, were called to this:

> The Lord himself has placed us like an example and a mirror, not only for others but for our sisters whom the Lord has also called to our way of life, so that they in their turn will be a mirror and example to those who live in the world. Therefore, since the Lord has called us to such greatness that those who are to be models and mirrors for others can see themselves mirrored in us, how greatly are we bound to bless the Lord, to praise him, more and more to be strengthened in him so that we do what is good. And

so, if we have lived according to the form of life we have been given, then, with very little effort, we shall leave others a noble example.[9]

Thus, in the full development of their thought on the Christian vocation, they took Christ's words quite literally, that whoever did the will of the Father, was Christ's own brother and sister, as well as his mother. They understood that it is the Holy Spirit who brings this about, just as it was the Spirit who had overshadowed Mary. Out of their reflections on this, grew their perception of the central place of the Spirit in our Christian lives. They often spoke of 'the Spirit of the Lord and his holy manner of working'. They recognised the Spirit as fruitful and creative, working in their own lives, in every life and in the whole of creation, just as within the Trinity, where the Spirit is the bond of love. This dynamic of love is so powerful that it assumes all that we mean by personhood, and it was this person, called the Spirit, who overshadowed Mary so that she became the Mother of the Lord. Her union with the Spirit was so complete that Christ, the 'icon of the Godhead', was made manifest in a way which was new in human history. This same Spirit overshadows us, uniting us to Christ with a union every bit as real and every bit as new.

Because the bridegroom was the description Christ used of himself, Francis felt it important to know what he meant and what he understood by it. How was he to think of himself as a bride? In time he was able to tell us: This, he says, is what it means to be a bride, when the faithful soul is united by the Holy Spirit to our Lord, Jesus Christ.[10] To be a bride is to be united by the bond of the Spirit, loving and fruitful. Here again, the paradigm is Mary. Like her, we find our fruitfulness in the creative Godhead, mediated to us through the Spirit, expressed by the humanity of Jesus. Francis had all this in mind when he wrote to Clare and said: You have made yourselves the beloved (the darling) of the Holy Spirit;[11] meaning that she and her community were wholly given to this transcendent and creative love, arguably the most powerful force in the universe.

The relations within the Trinity, as Francis describes them, do not always unravel in a one-to-one way, so that we cannot say: Francis saw this as belonging to the Father, this to the Bridegroom, this to the Spirit. Francis well understood that all

God's works are works of unity, springing from wholeness, and that everything created is a parable and revelation of the uncreated God. As a result, Francis uses words like Father or Mother to mean the Father, Christ or the Spirit, according to the dynamic of the moment. Even though he consistently uses the pronoun 'He' of God, his thinking was not in any way chauvinist in the modern sense. His perceptions of God soar off into stuttering attempts to utter the Godhead in human words:

> You are goodness, beauty, peace, refreshment, justice, strength, sweetness, hope, life, all good, strong, holy, great, living, true, meekness, moderation . . . [12]
>
> He is merciful and gentle, holy and right . . . holy, just, true . . . all pardon, all grace, all glory . . . without beginning and end, without change, invisible, beyond description, beyond words, beyond understanding . . . most high, gentle, lovable, delightful and more than everything else, wholly desirable for ever.[13]

Francis and Clare knew that they—and we—were caught up into this life within the Godhead itself. In a certain sense, they made no attempt to understand it but simply accepted that the words of the Gospel meant what they said. For this reason, they laid down that, for the brothers and sisters, the rule of life is the holy Gospel and the teaching of our Lord Jesus Christ.[14] The Gospel is all, no more is needed. Their uncomplicated observance of the Gospel led Clare to an intense and almost mystical union with God, and it led Francis to the mountain of La Verna and a physical identification with Christ which we call the stigmata.

They often meditated on how

> the most High Father, in heaven announced this Word of the Father—so worthy, so holy and glorious—in the womb of the holy and glorious Virgin Mary, from whom he [the Word] received the flesh of humanity and our frailty; and though he was rich beyond all other things in this world he, together with the most blessed virgin, his mother, willed to choose poverty.[15]

When they read all this and pondered on it, their own way forward seemed quite clear. When Francis spoke about living in poverty and following the poverty of Christ, we might wonder whether he saw this as something to which a small, élite, group were called, or whether he saw it as something to which every Christian was summoned. Part of the answer to this question is implicit in the fact that not only does he spell this out in his Rule for his brothers and his Form of Life for Clare and her sisters, but also in his *Letter to All the Faithful*. On the other hand, this Letter was written as a guideline, to be given to those who asked for it. We can conclude from this that he saw a commitment to poverty as a response to some prior stirring in the heart of which the person had already become aware. He did not see it as the practice of an élite and dedicated few, but his many propertied friends testify to the fact that he never told them they were wrong to have house or lands. He never slipped into the trap of suggesting that property was wrong (although some of his followers have done) but to anyone who asked him what they should do, he repeated the words of the Gospel: If you wish to be perfect, go and sell what you have and give it to the poor and then come and follow me;[16] but he also accepted that not everyone felt called to anything so radical. It was not his way to tell others what they should be doing. The Gospel was there for all to read. His task was to be a herald, to announce the Good News and to recall people to conversation and prayer. Who knows, he might have said, what God is planning?

Who knows indeed? Francis and Clare had both discovered that the work of God far exceeds our wildest imaginings. Like the universe, we were marvellously created out of nothing. They saw that we have absolutely nothing of our own, but that it is only in our nothingness that we have a space big enough for God. Our problem is that we find this too painful, so we tend to fill our lives with other things, buffers against reality. Francis realised, very early on, that when he found this truth of his nothingness so painful, it was because his value system had become upside-down and so the more he struggled, the more he was wrenching things out of true. His sin, from the beginning, had been his determination to be the centre of the universe, to 'exalt himself over all the good things which the Lord says and does in him'.[17] When he followed God's advice and took 'the bitter for the sweet', he entered upon a more accurate, because more God-like, value system.

Like him, we need to struggle with our false values. We, too, find it hard to receive everything as a gift, not only because we like to own things, but also because we like to have security of tenure. We want to be sure about the future. This is our timidity, our smallness of heart and our penury. Redemption will come alive in us when we consent to have this penury changed into poverty, a transformation set in motion by our choice of 'his own most glorious Self'. Francis said that we became alienated from our true poverty when, in the beginning, we 'lost our wisdom'[18] and it was out of this rediscovered wisdom that Clare spoke when she sang her praises of poverty:

> O blessed poverty
>   giving eternal riches to those who love and choose her;
> O holy poverty,
>   to those who hold you and long for you
>   God has promised the kingdom of heaven
>   and most certainly granted eternal glory and blessed
>   life!
> O tender poverty,
>   which the Lord Jesus Christ,
>   who has ruled and still rules heaven and earth,
>   who spoke and things were made,
>   preferred and chose to embrace before all else![19]

So for Francis and Clare, poverty was a doorway into God. They chose to be poor in order to be like Christ and his mother, and so to restore the right order of things. God is the Most High, creator of all, giver of all; they were the little, poor ones whom the Lord had called,[20] and both sides of that definition are equally important. Let us refer everything to God, said Francis, and confess that everything good is his, and thank him for everything, for all good comes from him.[21]

If we do this, we will 'come to hold him who holds everything together', for we are meant to begin loving and living with God now. We are not meant to spend our whole lives getting our act together as a preliminary; we learn how to live and move and have our being in God, as we go along. Mary did not say to the angel: I'm not ready, wait a bit, but: Let it be done. In the same way, we are called to become brothers, sisters and mothers of Christ in each other, now. By our love, we bring the life of Christ to birth within each other's hearts. We bear him as truly as Mary did when we serve each other with courtesy and love. This awesome miracle will not be brought about by the conviction of our minds, but by the influence of love in our hearts. This is harder for us, because love is not subject to control, or at least, not to control by us, so love is always a risk. We seek alternatives; it is often easier to speculate about the truth, for instance, than to be willing to love irritating people. This last may even seem beyond us, but often the problem is that we do not want to love them, rather than that they are unlovable. Yet if we wait silently in God's presence, open to being transformed, even this transformation will come. Although we try to, we cannot choose the arena of our conversion; God insistently works within reality, while for us this is often the one thing we instinctively evade. Yet redemption, conversion, contrition, communion can only come to meet us where we are at any given moment.

It is interesting that for the extrovert Francis, the painful arena of his conversion drama was within, and the external changes fitted around it. Clare, on the other hand, who was a more introverted character, found the pain of her conversion focusing on the external acts through which she left home and moved towards life at San Damiano. This suggests a logical but unwelcome reflection: that our conversion must engage those aspects of ourselves which we would rather not know about. God's grace constantly leads towards the fullness of being, as Christ himself said: I am come that you may have life in abundance. The paradox of Christian living is that the path to life leads through death. This can equally well mean crossing the dead areas of ourselves, as Francis did in the pit, or dying to all we hold dear, as Clare did when she crept out of her home at night, or when hordes of angry uncles and cousins descended on San Paolo to force her back, or when—years later—Francis himself died and the brothers brought his body for her to see for the last time. Yet out of these deaths was born serenity and gentleness, ardour, tenderness, compassion and, above all, the ability to give life to others. These were the fruits of the Spirit of the Lord and his holy manner of working, and the same Tree can bear the same fruit for us. As the *Cloud of Unknowing* put it, all our life now must stand in desire. We must not meddle and think we know best; it is the Lord's work. To stand in desire means to wait, like Mary, asking: How can all this happen? It means being ready to struggle with new spiritual skills and allowing our perspectives and our values to change so that we are at God's disposal in peace and receptivity.

Jung relates how he showed some photographs of themselves to men in Africa who had never seen photographs before and how, at first, they were quite unable to find themselves in the black and white patterned oblong. It was a skill they lacked and had to learn. We are like that with God. We have to learn him and we can only do this by being with him and spending time in his company. This is the meaning of conversion and contrition—learning God over and over again, a different lesson each time. Meanwhile God acts as if we knew him well. This confuses us because we tend to see knowing and being known as two separate events rather than as one reciprocal, cyclic communication. God relentlessly relates to us just as we relentlessly speak to children until they have learnt the language. From a frame of reference which is quite different from our own, God continually speaks to us. Ignatius of Antioch said that he felt a spring bubbling up within him and murmuring: Come; not stridently shouting at him, but gently and continuously murmuring, like the welling of a small stream in a meadow, but ceaselessly—the relentless communication of God.

However we might rationalise it, we are basically afraid of this God who strangely likes us. The gentleness and understanding of God disconcert us and reveal how much our ideas are based on projections from within. We see God as judgemental because we are judgemental, destructively passionate because we are, demanding and totalitarian because we are, yet the Lord was not in the whirlwind but in the still, small voice which followed. The whirlwind is our stamping ground.

We are afraid of the fullness of life too, because we cannot imagine such a thing and feel that we do not know how to live in it. Our encounters with God reveal that our natural drift is into negativity and non-being, so the fullness of life looks to us like a dangerous activity and we fear being fully alive just as we fear anything else we cannot imagine. Our generalised uncertainty is made worse by our guilty awareness that the fullness of life, which we are not sure that we want, is a gift given to us at great cost. To learn to live gladly, so that everything is ours only as a gift and all our security is in God, is indeed to live at risk. It is also what Francis and Clare mean by being poor.

Francis tells us that we must keep in our hearts the good things the Lord reveals to us and make them manifest to others by our actions.[22] In other words, the way God has worked with us should be the pattern for our workings with others. 'Love one another as I have loved you,' said Christ. 'Do whatever he tells you,' said his mother (John 13:34; 2:5). Christ also said that we will be known by our fruits which will reveal what we really are. 'What we are before God, that we are and nothing more,' Francis used to say, meaning that we are what God sees us to be, but also meaning that unless we live in God's presence, we are nothing and nowhere, we are in exile from ourselves. Our true self is hidden in Christ, and we are kept in exile by the attachments and compulsions which drive us. These attachments are like an addiction. They retain their power over us because, even though we may hate them, we are used to them. Our greatest sickness can be that on the whole we prefer what we are used to, even if it means being sick. This is why Jesus Christ could say: The truth will set you free. Every compulsive attachment generates a slanted vision, a kind of squint, which damages our emotions by tugging them out of true. When we are freed from an attachment, the truth is restored to us, even if there is still quite a lot of healing needed to restore those emotions to an easy flow. They are, to change the metaphor, like muscles which have adjusted to a malformation and now have to be straightened out, and this process is often the most painful of all.

There are also the spiritual consequences of attachments which need to be healed. The spiritual damage we receive from them usually lies in the subtle attractions of power without responsibility. We choose to be greedy, lustful and selfish because we like what these things bring us, but we give no thought (or no effective thought) to their consequences for ourselves or others. Because of the element of choice involved and because our will, as well as our woundedness, maintains our attachments, letting go of them can be like dying. For the attachment itself it is a dying, since it will have gathered psychic energy to itself and can seem almost to take on an existence of its own. When we make our first, feeble attempts at liberation, this energy will rear up to defend itself. To let it die is part of what Christ meant when he spoke about losing our life in order to save it. We must lose the things we fasten on to because we think them essential to our lives, so that we can save the true life which we live in God.

Clare tells us that what we need to do here is to look at

Christ. We are cold and need to present ourselves to the sun for warming as lizards do. Christ is our sun. To look at Christ is to see hope, affirmation and encouragement because we see in him all the beauty of a humanity which we slowly realise to be *our* humanity. Unless we look upon Christ, we can fall into the way of thinking that our humanity is precisely our trouble, but when we gaze on him, we begin to understand that our trouble is just the opposite, that we are not yet human. We are not called to deny but to become what we are—living people, God's glory. Beyond that, we are invited to be his mother, bringing glory to birth in the hearts of others, both those we know and those beyond our knowing. 'Therefore, rejoice over and over again, and be glad, be filled with tremendous joy and spiritual happiness.'[23]

PART 3

Communion

Brother Francis and Sister Clare

Francis said that in the beginning, when he was first called by God, the Lord gave him brothers, and he always saw this call to be a brother as his primary call. He so explored and developed this idea that in the end he felt in loving relationship with everyone and everything. All that is made was a dear member of his family, every single creature his brother or sister, every stone and stream and tree, his home. He spoke of Brother Sun and Sister Moon, Brother Wind and Sister Water, Brother Fire and Mother Earth, and even of Sister Death. Towards the end of his life he wrote a song, giving praise to God through each of them and asking:

> Let everything you have made
> be a song of praise to you,
> above all, His Excellency the Sun (our brother);
> through him you flood our days with light.
> He is so beautiful, so radiant, so splendid,
> O Most High, he reminds us of you.
>
> My Lord, be praised
> through our Sister the Moon and through each Star.
> You made them so clear and precious and lovely
> and set them in the heavens for all to see.
>
> Through Brother Wind and Sister Water,
> Through Brother Fire and Mother Earth,
> Through Sister Death—be praised, O Lord,
> be praised.

Our kinship with all creation was a deeply held conviction for Francis, it was not just a poetic way of speaking, and he was always genuinely distressed when other species were treated or spoken to without respect. It was his own custom to speak to all creatures as if they knew Italian: Sing, Sister Cricket; come to me, Brother Rabbit; praise God, Sister Lark, he said; and in response, intuitive creation understood his message, if not his words. Animals and plants greeted him lovingly, welcomed his caresses and obeyed his commands. This is what Celano had in mind when he said that in his opinion, Francis had regained primitive innocence. Through grace, he had returned to, or come to, a condition in which there was no violence or division within him, nor, as a result, with any other. The animals and birds quickly sensed this and responded; more than that, they were willing to submit to his direction, take his advice and be obedient to him. Francis put a high value on obedience and was himself a deeply obedient man, though his superiors sometimes found his interpretations of it to be all his own. The story is told, for instance, that he had been forbidden to give away any more of his clothes to poorer men, and when a beggar asked him for his habit, for the love of God, he obediently related this but added that no one had forbidden the beggar to drag his habit off him. This solution satisfied them both.

As he himself grew more and more given to God, everything else gradually fell into place around him. This was the patient work of years in which he slowly learnt the right pattern of things. He learnt not to be afraid of mistakes, of looking silly or of denying common sense, so much so that, on one occasion, he refused to allow the brothers to put out the fire which was scorching his clothes. 'Do not harm our Brother Fire', he said, and although the brothers disobeyed him, it was 'against Francis' will'.[1] He had a great love for fire, which he said God had given us to light up the night when the sun was no longer shining. What he was struggling with is something which we all find difficult, namely, how do we maintain a sensible balance when we try to give the rest of creation its (long-denied) rights? He went so far as to say that a friar should be subject even to the wild beasts[2] so that they may do what they want with him. Yet his own life indicates to us that this struggle is only half the picture; we find the right balance when, through holiness, the other half comes into play, as it did for him. Once, when Francis was seriously ill with an eye disease and the doctor decided to cauterise the flesh of his face from ear to eyebrow, Celano tells us that he said to the red-hot flames of Brother Fire: 'The Most High has made you strong,

beautiful and useful. Be kind to me in this hour, and cour-
teous, for I have loved you in the past in the Lord.'[3] The
other brothers could not bear to watch the cauterising and ran
away, but Francis peacefully insisted that his brother Fire had
dealt gently with him and that he had felt no particular pain
from the brand.

This bears out something which will be even more apparent
when we come to consider the stigmata, namely that the
destructive element of pain (particularly physical pain) is not
in the cause of suffering, but in our resistance to it, that pain
and its consequences can be two different things. Francis
seems to have come to such inner wholeness that shattering
events were themselves broken against the rock of his integrity. He was receptive to everything that happened to him, but
invaded by nothing. He carried the message of the incarnation
to the same extreme of logic as St Paul, namely that every
aspect of human living is now filled with the presence of God,
'even sin'. He grieved about, and struggled with, his own
sinfulness, but as time went on he seems to have accepted it
with increasing simplicity and peace, and to have felt that on
the whole there were more important things to think about,
like how wonderful, good, beautiful and holy God is. He lived
with his sinfulness as with a constant in his equation which
could not be ignored, but which was far from being the beauty
of mathematics. For example, when Sister Cricket used to sing
for him every day at his request, he said, after about a week,
that he could find grounds in her behaviour for pride and self-
glorification, so he peacefully let her go her way. He knew
about his sin, but he was not attached to it and did nothing to
nourish it.

However, coming to terms with his own sin and weakness
was only one stage of his journey to integrity. He also had to
make his peace with the sinfulness of his brethren. At one
time, after he had resigned as Minister General but seeing
how things had deteriorated within the Order, he did what
Moses had done with the Israelites and handed the whole lot
back to God in despair. The Lord replied by asking Francis
whose work the Order was anyway, where did the grace of
conversion come from, and added that for every brother who
left it, another would be sent to take his place—'If he is not yet
born, I will see to it that he is.'[4] Eventually Francis realised
that his part was faithfully and peacefully to do what he had

undertaken, and to pray constantly that the Order would be protected and governed by God. When the brothers said to him: Why don't you do something? he would reply that all those other brethren had the Gospel and the Rule which they had all sworn to keep. In other words, the responsibility was theirs and even if one should rise from the dead . . .

It seems as if Francis had to come to a loss of power on every level. He resigned from being Minister General of his Order of his own choice, partly through sickness, partly with a feeling that government of that sort was beyond him, in some degree with a feeling of failure. He was torn apart by the dissensions among the brothers and by the endless arguments about poverty and the Rule. All he had wanted, and all he had felt called to do, was to live with a group of brothers who simply observed the Gospel as it stands, '*sine glossa*' as he used to say, without commentaries to explain and explain away.

Towards the last years of his life, he also became chronically ill and the cures of the time seem to have made him worse. When he had his eye cauterised, he was already almost blind, generally sick and debilitated. Wounded in body and spirit by the stigmata, burdened with a suffering way out of the normal range of human endurance, he was unable to walk or do very much for himself; yet out of this far-reaching diminishment, from the darkness of a small, rat-infested hut near San Damiano, came his radiant song about the beauty of creation and his love for all that had been made. It is a song preoccupied with the visual: the brightness of light, the rich colours of flowers, the glory of fire at night, the beauty of sun, moon and stars. There is not a trace of self-pity that he can no longer see them. The important thing for Francis was what God had done, not what he, Francis, had benefited from.

Praise and glory, honour and blessing
Be yours, O Lord,
O Most High,
O Most Powerful.

Praise and glory, honour and blessing
Be yours, O Most High.
O my Lord, be praised.

Let everything you have made
be a song of praise to you,
above all, His Excellency the Sun (our brother);
through him you flood our days with light.
He is so beautiful, so radiant, so splendid,
O Most High, he reminds us of you. . . .

Let everything you have made
be a song of praise to you.
above all, our Sister, our Mother, Lady Earth
who feeds and rules and guides us.
Through her you give us fruits and flowers
rich with a million hues.
O my Lord, be praised.

We are told that he later added some verses about forgiveness
when the Bishop and the Mayor had a row and Francis was
able to bring them to reconciliation:

Be praised, my Lord,
through those who forgive for your love,
through those who are weak,
in pain, in struggle,
who endure with peace,
for you will make them Kings and Queens
O Lord Most High.

and one about death when he realised that his own was near.

Through Death, O Lord, be praised,
through our Sister Death,
our Sister Death of the body.
No one who lives can escape from Sister Death.
How terrible for those who have died already from sin;
How blest for those who are alive in Your most holy will,
no further death can harm them.

In this song Francis, from his physically reduced situation,
reflects on the wonders that God has made in our everyday
world and makes his own statement about their relative
values. We see here, to an acute degree in Francis, something
which is familiar to us from the life of almost every artist, but
which we may not expect to find as a part of our own life of
prayer, and that is the creative interplay of pain and beauty,

the chiaroscuro of a light and dark which is moral and spiritual as well as physical. Everywhere we can see that it is the
shadow which reveals the light. The light is invisible to us
unless its absence reveal it. In the same way, none of us understands the place of suffering and sin in life, but none of us can
consider Christ and deny their centrality. We are bewildered
by the way that 'even sin' works for good through the hands
of God, but is this, we can ask, the same thing in another
dimension — that the light is invisible unless the shadow reveal
it?

Our position is no longer simply the one Paul describes,
whereby we do what we do not want, and fail to do what we
want. Instead of that, like Francis, we will be led into situations where life and death are no longer so clearly separated,
nor perhaps so distinct. There is a drawing by Maurice Escher
in which black swans fly over a light ground on one side of the
page, and gradually change until white swans are flying over a
black ground on the other side. Just so do light and dark, life
and death modulate within us, until we come to suspect that
at root they are intimately connected — and we realise that, of
course, this is exactly the statement of the resurrection. Death
seems inimical (or desirable) to us because we perceive it as
disintegration, but our Christian experience reveals that there
is within us a life of joy not patient of destruction:

> How blest for those who are alive in Your most holy will,
> no further death can harm them.

This whole song is Francis' relationship with God set out in
words, filled with the distilled essence of his prayer. It shows
how everything was, for him, a living letter from God, every
element of creation spoke to him of the one who created it. It
reveals how he realised creation's call to sing constant praise
to God:

> Let everything you have made
> be a song of praise to you.

Through the sun and moon and stars, through the clouds and
water and earth and each other's good example ('those who
forgive for your love') God is praised and honoured, and we
are led to God by them. In consequence, he saw the footprints
of God everywhere. From everything that is made, he learnt
more about the way God, who made us all, who intends us to

live together in our shared world. So he learnt from creation the inner meaning of his call to be a brother. This was his vocation, all the rest was commentary.

Angelo, Leo and Rufino, 'we who were with him', tell a story which had taken place some years earlier, but which delicately illustrates Francis' understanding of how we should relate to each other. It is a story about a cricket who lived near his cell, 'the last cell near the hedge of the garden behind the house where Brother Rayner the gardener lived after Francis' death'[5] they say precisely. This cricket sheltered in a fig tree and used, Celano maintains, to 'sing sweetly'. Francis would call the cricket to come to him and hold out his hand for her to sit on. She would climb along his finger and let him stroke her, and at his request would sing, chirping on until Francis too joined in and sang. This happened, not once, but daily for a whole week, whenever he went out of his cell and called her. He would study the cricket, discerning her inner nature and sensitively opening himself to her secret, as he did with everyone. We considered earlier the way in which gazing with an open heart generates love in us, and here we see an example of it. It seems that Francis not only loved creatures for God's sake, but he learnt to love them as God loves them, tenderly and with delight. 'He discerned their hidden nature with his sensitive heart', and so the timid knew they were safe with him and 'even cruel things were made gentle'—like the fire.

Order was so completely restored within him that his presence restored others to harmony; it was part of his gift of being a brother that others could share in all that God had given him. His poverty freed him to be generous, his obedience gave him the right, and the power even, to command the birds and animals. After some struggle ('Don't honour me too soon', he said, 'I may yet have a wife and children'), he had become a chaste man, with all the implications of integrity which we have already considered; he had 'returned to primitive innocence'. He not only saw what God sees, but he saw as God sees. In consequence, he was like the man in the Gospel whose eye was full of light, the splinters removed as well as the plank, and like Ruth to Naomi, he could say to God: Your people shall be my people.[6]

No person was too small for his careful attention. He would remove worms from the path in case anyone trampled on them and said several times that the bees were to be cared for during the winter, insisting that they had honey and the best wine to tide them over. Everything he saw reminded him of God. The worm on the path symbolised Christ who, through the psalm, spoke of himself as a worm and not a man; it was also a lesson to Francis about a degree of vulnerability and surrender to events which he felt he had not yet attained; but the worm was also Francis' brother, a brother dependent on others for protection from the destructive hazards to which worms, as we, are subject.

His reading of Genesis never led Francis to see himself as lord and master of the animals and plants. He did not even consider himself God's steward with regard to creation, because he did not consider he was 'over' anyone or anything, even in a delegated capacity. At all times, he was a brother, and in so far as he was charged with anything, it was with the privilege of caring for creation in a loving and brotherly way. As a result of this attitude, there was nothing exploitative or greedy or manipulative in his approach.

He gave the brethren good, ecologically sound advice about the use of natural resources. He told them to leave a border around their gardens which had not been dug over, so that the grass and flowers might have somewhere to bloom and proclaim God's beauty. He used to insist that special places be set aside for herbs and flowering plants. He never wanted to terminate the life of anything and forbade the brothers to cut down the whole tree when they cut wood for the fire, because the tree, too, must be allowed the hope of sprouting again. This was not sentimentality but a deep and respectful awareness that nothing existed just for him, as if he were the owner in some way. Rather, he saw the dying and rising of Christ as the basic story, the foundation event of our planet, and possibly of the universe, and that everything which exists does so within these parameters of Christ. The trees, too, must be left with hope of their resurrection. Christ's story is our story and that of our planet, and by our lives, we re-tell it over and over again. We have no right to bring this story to closure in any of its myriad versions.

Clare says very much the same sort of things in her Testament where she lays down that any land the sisters have, over and above what they need for growing their food, should not be cultivated or planted but left untouched and undeveloped.[7] In her Rule, she says that it may be made into a garden for the sisters, but both texts make it clear that this land is not to be used for gain or profit in any way. The land, too, has rights and is not to be exploited.

She and Francis considered it a corollary of being brother and sister that they only took what they needed from the soil; after that it must be left to sing its own song about the glory of God. They were not addicted to 'usefulness' and had no problem with tracts of land not being productive. Wild flowers, butterflies and mice shared the world with Friars and Poor Ladies, they were not chance denizens but members of the family. When Clare sent sisters out on necessary business she would remind them to praise God for the beauty of the trees, the flowering plants and bushes, as well as for all the people they might meet.[8] Francis and Clare both knew that the earth depends on us to care for it and when Clare considered the small piece of land around San Damiano, she sought to bring it to fulfilment on its own terms, not on ours. She fully realised that redemption is effected by enabling each thing to become what God meant it to be.

This was all included in Celano's phrase about Francis sensitively discerning the hidden nature of things. It was also included in Francis and Clare's contemplative stance, or attitude, which accepted and honoured the individuality of each creation, was open to know it in its depths and eager to learn about God from everything that is made. 'The most high, heavenly Father chose to enlighten my heart', she tells us.[9] This enlightenment showed her that God is in everything, the source and origin which we all share. It was her awareness of shared beginnings which made her sister to all.

Clare's earliest experience of being sister, was of course in her relationship with Agnes of Assisi, not to be confused with Agnes of Prague to whom the letters were written. Agnes of Assisi was Clare's next sister. She certainly had one other, Beatrice, who also joined her at San Damiano and was later sent to France on foundation, and possibly a third, as some of the witnesses at the Canonisation Process were identified as Clare's nieces. The *Life of Clare* tells us that although they had always been very close, it was only when Clare had left home and began to pray seriously for Agnes to follow her, that a 'marvellous mutual love took hold of them both'.[10] Obviously Clare hoped to influence her younger sister and realised her responsibility to make this influence good. Now she prayed that the 'affinity of spirit' which they had always had, might become 'unity of will in the service of God'. This prayer was abundantly answered and Agnes was to live at San Damiano for some years, witnessing many of Clare's miracles, and she was also to be present at her death. In between she had been sent to establish the Poor Clare life in Florence, an exile which she felt keenly: '[I] suffer great distress and immense sadness because I have been physically separated from you and my other sisters with whom I had hoped to live and die. This distress has a beginning but it knows no end', she wrote.[11] Many of us are cautious about giving our hearts to that extent and there is no doubt that when we finally open ourselves to others, we run a terrible risk of vulnerability. Francis and Clare well understood why we keep the drawbridge up, but they also knew that being a true brother or sister involved letting it down, genuinely welcoming the other into our inner keep. It means more than 'putting up with each other for Christ's sake'; it means the readiness to live together with real feelings of liking, to be friends together, to encourage each other in doing good. It has nothing in common with sentimentality or the fear of upsetting the other. If Agnes could write so vehemently from Florence, one wonders how she had reacted when the idea of going there had first been mooted, but obviously Clare had not shrunk from it on that score, nor had she softened the edges in any way. This was not because she was hard but because she understood that the first person to whom we are sister and brother is Christ himself. Whatever the physical relationship, it is in Christ that we find our primary relationship, and so the work of Christ, which is the work of the Father, must be the top priority in all situations. This is why Francis used to call Clare Christiana, the Christian, because he saw her as a true sister of Christ, our brother.

In their depositions at the Canonisation Process, the sisters were full of stories about Clare's sisterly care, both for themselves and for those who came to visit the monastery. She seemed especially concerned with children and with food. They say that she never got irritable or agitated—in itself probably grounds for canonisation. She was always gentle and loving, though often very challenging, for example in her blunt speaking to a man who had thrown his wife out many years before, though at the same time she prayed that it be made easier for him to do as she suggested. Some who were sick she would heal with the sign of the Cross, to others she would give advice. If they sinned, 'astonishingly, she wept' they tell us.[12] We see in her as in Francis, the same acceptance for everyone, at once uncritical but uncompromising.

We have already noted that the hallmark of true prayer appears, not in ecstasy or rapture, but in daily life. The way Francis and Clare lived out their call to be brother and sister suggests that we can now push that statement a little further and say that prayer is not only what happens in the time of prayer, but that there is no time which is not prayer. In their daily life, they were always open to the mystery of God present in their midst. God was around them like the air, and no matter how preoccupied their minds, their hearts were aware; this gave them a holiness which, one of the sisters said at the Canonisation Process, she could not fully explain. They never ceased to adore and be amazed, not with a kind of stream of consciousness, talking away to God beneath the daily flow of things, giving only half their minds and hearts to those around them, but rather by the music within them playing in harmony with the music they heard around them. Prayer is worship more than anything else, and the lover of God knows how to find God in the strangest places. They were brother and sister to everything and everyone, and as they lived this out in daily life, Clare and Francis worshipped the God who is Father and Mother of all that is.

8

An Incarnation of the Incarnation

Two years before his death, Francis was led into the wilderness by the Spirit. Celano tells us that he had come to an extraordinary degree of familiarity with God and had been given a taste of God in a way which is quite rare.[1] Like everyone who truly loves, he longed for complete union, an end to all separations and separateness, to be wholly given to the one he loved. Not all of us love God like that, and we may not even aspire to, but when we read about it we catch a glimpse of a mountain peak and guess that from it, the view would be wonderful beyond imagining. Though it may not last, briefly we long to come there. St Teresa of Avila used to say that it is right to have great desires, that we cannot be too bold with God, no matter how poor a thing we feel ourselves to be. She said this to encourage us though we may often feel it more as a reproach that we are not, on the whole, bothered by the audacity of our desires in God's regard.

Out in the wilderness, Francis, whose desires were infinite, took the book of the Gospel into the little chapel of his hermitage and placed it on the altar. He asked God to show him what more he could do to complete the work already begun. He then stood up, made the sign of the Cross and opened the Gospels. From the trouble Celano takes to tell us that other saints and most perfect men have done the same, we conclude that he was a little unsure about this procedure. Francis did it several times in his life and trustingly shaped his actions around the answers, but Celano never quite shed his desire that his loved and admired Francis should be seen as a proper, conventional saint. Francis' own position was quite simple, the Bible was the Word of God. If he wanted to know what God was saying to him, then he opened the Bible, though he seems to have done so only at turning points in his life, not every time he had a small decision to make. For these he would pray for guidance: We must ask God's advice about this, he used to say.

In spite of Celano's ambivalence, we can still hear through his account how moved Francis was at the message given by the text. All the years of struggle were now bearing this fruit, that he stood before the God of Fire like dry tinder, the words of the Word open in his hands. The first thing he read was that he would suffer tribulation. He opened the book again and then again, and each time came to the same passage. He was quite unshaken by these promises, in fact, he sang with happiness. As much as anything else, it is the way Francis sings about God when he is happy which brings home to us how much God had become part of his life. God was not a dimension apart, nor someone he related to only in prayer and higher moments, but rather, so much a part of the everyday things as to pervade all his human gifts of loving, feeling and relating. From God he received what he gave so abundantly to others, humans and animals: the gift of self-transcendence, of doing 'better than their best', of being greater than themselves through the energy of another's love. He knew where he had placed his trust and although he approached God with awe, he also approached with familiarity and ease and, quite simply, happiness.

Some time later, again while he was praying, he saw a man standing above him, at first glance reminiscent of the seraphim of Isaiah. Each seraph in the vision of Isaiah had 'six wings: two to cover its face, two to cover its feet and two for flying' (Isa. 6:2). In the vision of Francis, the focus of attention is not so much on the winged aspect of the seraph, itself a symbol of mysterious divinity, but on the way in which the vision seemed to shift between being a seraph and being human, being Christ in fact. We are told that the hands were stretched out and nailed to a cross, and the feet were joined together and nailed, too. So the vision was primarily of Christ crucified, not exactly of the risen Christ but of a Christ whose human wounds had been absorbed into the life of the Godhead, symbolised by the seraph.

Part of our trouble here is that nobody really knows what a seraph is like or even what a seraph is. The noun is an English form of a Latin form of a Hebrew word, of which the root is uncertain but perhaps refers to burning in the sense of stinging, like the fiery serpents in Numbers 21. With the passage of time and the input of various schools of mystical thought, the word has acquired overtones of meaning more connected with burning in love, and seraphim are thought to be the spirits nearest to God's throne and therefore 'highest' and most ardent. So they have become symbols of a supreme form of love, blazing unimaginably, like the burning bush of Moses, aflame but never consumed. In Francis' vision, not only were the hands stretched out and nailed to a cross and the feet joined together and nailed, but two wings of the seraph were stretched up above his head, two were extended as if for flight and two were wrapped around the whole body. So the vision was both of Christ crucified and Christ-God, for Francis had asked to share in the pain of the Passion, as far as he was able, but he had also asked to share, as far as he was able, in the love which drove and motivated Christ throughout his Passion. This had been his answer to himself when he had asked what more could he do, when he had 'gazed' at Christ, in Clare's word, and realised what we all find, that there is always a beyond with God into which we are invited but never ordered. For Francis at this moment, the beyond took the form of further initiation into redemptive love and the pain of it.

This vision was God's response to Francis' plea, a response in the form of an image which summed up the whole mystery of God made human. The vision shows us that pain and redemption interlock, which we dimly guess, but it also shows something which we adumbrate in theory but shrink from in practice, that within the Godhead there is such great delight and joy in love, that all the sufferings of all the world cannot extinguish it. This does not mean that our sufferings do not matter or that they are trivial, although that is often what we feel it to mean. Indeed, the image of Christ as love in pain, spells out for us that our suffering is greatly honoured by God, that our pain is received with reverence and taken right into the being of the Godhead and somehow made a part of that divine life. The truth remains, though, that unquenchable joy is the essence of God, that is what God is, and, to speak anthropomorphically, God makes adjustments to integrate pain—just as we do. Within God is the spring of all delight which could only cease if God ceased. That pain and delight can dwell together, is revealed to us in this vision of Francis', which is part of its relevance to each of us. It is yet another clear reiteration that by Christ's becoming what we are, we are invited to share what God is. No explanations are offered, only the fact of burning love and the fact of pain. The seraph expresses both poles, the divine love in the radiant, mysterious being, and the human pain in the crucified figure. It brings them together, a harbinger of the new heaven and the new earth. It shows us Christ, the first-born of many. It shows us the herald of the new creation speaking to the herald of the Great King.

When Francis rose up from his vision, he felt filled with joy at the way the seraph had looked at him, and filled with fear of the nails and the sharpness of the suffering in the vision. He rose to his feet 'sorrowful and joyful'. As he struggled to come to terms with what he had seen and to understand what meaning it might have for him, the marks of the nails slowly began to appear in his own hands and feet, just as he had seen them a little while before in the crucified seraph. Finally his hands and feet seemed to be pierced through, the heads of the nails showed on the palms of his hands and the tops of his feet, while on the other side their pointed ends could be seen, bent and driven back and raised above the flesh.

It is very difficult for us to know what to make of this. Since Francis' time there have been a number of people who carried the stigmata, the wounds of Christ, on their bodies, but if, as seems likely, Francis was the first, it must have been a profound shock to him on every level, with ramifications right through daily life. Padre Pio, asked if the wounds hurt, replied dryly that God had not given them to him for a joke. When we look at Francis' behaviour after the event, we see a man showing all the symptoms of extreme shock, of someone struggling to come to terms with the unthinkable. He covers the wounds up, avoids the problems they create, refuses to talk about it, can be quite sharp with those who try to force a discussion. When one brother asked what they were, Francis pointed to his eye and said that if this looked like an eye, then that is what it was, and left the brother to make what he could of that answer. For a time, he almost seemed to behave like someone in deep depression and it is only when we know what was burning in his heart, that we realise how untrue this was.

In spite of the many ways in which this experience of Francis' might seem to have little relevance to the everyday Christian trying to pray in an everyday way, there are several reasons why the stigmata of Francis do indeed have something to say to us. Every one who follows Christ is called to be his presence in the world, called to become Christ-like and invited to put on Christ, in so far as they are able. As we move further into our life of prayer, in depth and in time, we increasingly realise that while we understand putting on Christ to refer to our struggle to live in a Christ-like way, grace is undeniably leading us into a much deeper modelling on the pattern of Christ's life. It is as if God understands putting on Christ with a literalism we are hardly able to imagine.

We may not see it while it is happening, but when we look back on our life of prayer we can sometimes see how the cosmic patterns of death and resurrection have been working themselves out, even in our small affairs. Great mysteries express themselves in amazingly everyday ways. Just as Christ was the Word made flesh, so we are invited to become the same: the love of the Godhead in bodily form, invited to continue speaking this message of love and communication. 'Love one another as I have loved you' and then 'we will come to you and make our home in you' (John 14:23). Christ is the first-born, the eldest, but only the first of many. We are the many. Like Francis, we gradually become incarnations of the incarnation. This is our calling.

Francis was aware that he had to fulfil part of his apostolic call by being an example for others to follow. This was why John the Simple rubbed his nose when Francis did and turned around when Francis did. This was what Clare meant when she talked about being a person in whom others could see Christ mirrored. We all have this responsibility to be seen striving to follow the Way we have professed as Christians. We need not succeed — our readiness to acknowledge failure is often of greater apostolic conviction than knowing the right answers. To form Christ in us is God's business, to be completed in God's time, and whether our likeness to Christ is great or still slight, it will be made manifest when the time requires it.

Celano tells us that although Francis hid the marks of Christ's wounds for a long time, even from his closest friends, yet divine providence did not intend that situation to go on and made sure that the marks were seen and, presently, understood. God revealed his work, as so often and to our constant surprise, through small practical things. The fact that the marks were on his hands and feet as well as on his side, made it very hard for Francis to conceal them for long. Everyone could see that he had trouble in walking and that he used to pull his sleeves down so that his hands were covered. His awkwardness when he came to wash was considerable and so—we are told—he only did so rarely! The wound in his side was in some ways easier to conceal, but, like the others, it bled constantly, and naturally the brothers at the laundry wondered about it. They could never get a straight answer from Francis, though they asked both directly and indirectly. Francis' silence sprang partly from the same self-knowledge that had made him send the cricket away after a few days; he knew what he was like and how quickly he could begin to exalt himself because of the works God had performed in him. He was afraid of the ease with which he could tarnish the wonders of God. Beyond that, what could one say about something so new and so extraordinary? How could one even begin to explain or comment or talk about such a thing?

In September 1224, he began to try, and opened his heart to Brother Leo his confessor, at the same time writing down some of the words which were filling his being:

> You are holy, you are the only Lord and God, you who work wonders.
>
> You are mighty. You are great. You are the Highest. You are the all-powerful King. You are the holy Father, King of heaven and earth.
>
> You are three and one, the Lord God of all gods. You are the good, the whole good, the greatest good, O Lord God, living and true.
>
> You are love, charity. You are wisdom. You are humility. You are patience. You are beauty. You are security. You are peace. You are joy and happiness. You are our hope. You are justice. You are temperance. You are the whole of our wealth.
>
> You are beauty. You are gentleness. You are the one who protects. You are our guard and our defence. You are strength. You are refuge.
>
> You are our hope. You are our faith. You are our love. You are all our sweetness. You are our everlasting life, O great and wonderful Lord, almighty God, merciful Saviour.

These are the words of someone who cannot express his over-flowing heart, of someone who has come to the great simplicity of wonder. They are not altogether what we might have expected, which is that he would have written a poem about his vision, or about the experience of receiving and bearing such wounds, telling about, or even talking to, Christ as he had seen him crucified in the seraph. Instead of this he speaks directly about God, in short, repetitive statements of amazement springing from the depths of his heart. We realise that what we have been given here are not the words of a man who has seen Christ, but the words of a man who sees as Christ sees. Not only has he put on Christ in a most literal physical way, but he has also put on Christ in his mind-set and his inner attitudes, as if, for a few moments, he had shared the view from the cross, seeing the world and God as Christ saw them, and out of that transforming insight speaks directly to the Godhead. 'You are holy. You are three in one. You are the greatest good.' God is beauty, all else is beautiful. God is wisdom, humility, patience; in God we become wise, humble and patient. God is life; we live.

It is as if Francis were no longer speaking as a 'stranger and pilgrim' (Eph. 2:19; 1 Pet. 2:11; Lev. 25:23) but from within the heart of the Trinity in some way, and for a moment we too are caught up and stand with him on the edges of the incomprehensible ocean which we so casually call God. His words surface from immersion in the All, the utterances of someone who has seen such richness that he might say the same thing over and over again, and yet mean something different each time. This is what Richard Rolle felt when he kept repeating: Burning love, Burning love; or Pascal when he wrote: Fire. Fire. Fire. Francis had come to the place where words limp and falter. We listen to the words of the Word; Francis on this occasion heard the Word itself speaking in silence.

To use his hymn ourselves, taking a phrase into our prayer or repeating it during the day, allows what Francis saw and said to seep into us, too, and his words to begin kindling in us the vanguard of their great heat. By prayerful repetition, they bring about the attitudes they sprang from, they generate in us what they expressed in Francis. They begin to lead us towards mystery, and with familiarity they seem less rather than more easy to grasp. We grow both more sure and less sure about what they mean, as we are led beyond the threshold of words towards infinite meaning. The inescapable truth is that God is mystery and everything we say about God is both true and not true at the same time. So the simplest words are best because they are the least wrong, but we do not really understand what Francis meant when he said that God is beauty, wisdom, love, all good. It becomes clear, too, that although Francis was (as we might think) in a position to know God better, yet he saw, more clearly than any of us, the wonder and incomprehensibility of God. The more he knew, the more he realised he knew nothing, while at the same time he loved more and suffered more deeply at his lack of love. Until then, he had taken the best words he knew, knowing that God was more. From now on, his real communication about God to us was his own, physical self. Just as Moses came back from Sinai with his face radiant from the sight of God, so Francis came back from La Verna with glowing flesh. His imitation of Christ was almost complete.

Yet it is also true that the experience of Francis is only a visual expression of something to which we are all called, for every Christian is invited to be an incarnation of the incarnation, every Christian effects a physical presence of Christ in the world. On the whole, we can rise to the concept of being brothers, sisters and even mothers of Christ, just as we are grateful when Christ works through us and uses us, but we are taken aback by the notion that we should become Christ, just as we are taken aback by the invitation to union with God. Our problem is that in spite of Christ we feel a great ambivalence before God about our humanity, and we resist both the notion of being sinners (although redeemed) and the notion of being redeemed (although sinful). Darkly, we suspect that God has cornered us. With even greater anxiety, we slowly realise that God has great hopes and desires for us. Most overturning of all is the realisation that, even though we are invited into a sharing of the divine, we are never summoned out of our original humanity. There is no suggestion that God might consider humanity a mistake, an experiment to be forgotten, a phase of our development which we can now leave behind with the help of grace. That might be the way we would handle the matter, but God, instead, issues this call to become Christ with all our weaknesses, aware that those weaknesses and our struggles with them, do not go away but remain to the end — no matter how Christ-like we might become. God, who is in what is, never denies reality, and a large part of our reality is the effect of the actions of sinful people (including ourselves). Francis' wounds indicate that the meaning of redemption is: God's glory entrusted to our fragility.

We may wonder what this experience had been like for

Francis, how it had felt to be so drawn beyond himself that he returned even looking like the Other. This had already been happening to him in smaller ways, right from the time when he had emerged from the cave 'so changed as to appear a different man'. Clearly his self-giving and self-surrender had here attained an ultimate quality, an echo of the total self-giving of the One he was imitating. There seem two obvious reflections on this: first that by and through the stigmata, Francis experienced something quantitatively, if not qualitatively, different from anything most of us ever know; and second that the nearest thing in most people's lives (almost the only experience we can take and say: it was this but infinitely more than this) is the experience of loving sexual union at its best. This makes good sense when we reflect that love and creativity are the activities in which we are most God-like. The well-known fact that in many human relationships we see the partners growing to resemble each other over the years, suggests that what happened to Francis was not so much utterly bizarre, as an intense example of something very familiar. We are more accustomed (or we think we are) to see this operating in human relationships than in our relationship with God, and for some reason we do not expect our human patterns of relating to function in connection with the one who is, after all, their prototype and origin. We must not fall into the trap of thinking that only Christ's humanity is loved by God, and we are only loved in so far as we are like Christ. God genuinely and personally loves all of us human beings and delights to be where we are. Christ remains all the things he said he was, a doorway, a path, a light for the journey, a guide, a shepherd, the beginning and the end, and so much more, but Christ is not a substitute for us. We have been loved ever since the story began.

This is both difficult to realise and difficult to respond to, not least because we are neither sure what love means in such a context, nor do we know how it is to be expressed. 'Good behaviour' alone cannot contain the whole of our response to the Infinite. For many people there is a real problem about the place of human feelings in our relationship with God. This can become acute, as we move out of the kind of spirituality in which we just 'say prayers' and into one where God becomes a presence and a longing in our lives, a person to be reckoned with. How do we express our love for our disembodied God, even for the risen Christ, when we ourselves are expressed in ambiguous bodies? Most of our relating takes place in the frame of our self-awareness as man or woman, but what do these terms mean when confronted by or confronting God? In our thinking about ourselves, our nature is inextricably intermingled with our gender, for it is our prime medium of interaction with others. Yet we are sheepish of being like this before God—who made us.

In relating to God, we think we should do so out of our higher selves, perhaps from the eyes upwards, but not as a man or woman learning new, spiritual skills of eternal love. This notion instantly suggests to us that our physical presence is somehow lower, and theology itself has not always been free from this view. In fact, ascetical theology has often said that feelings do not matter, what matters is doing the right thing at the right time; burning with love is all right for mystics but a bit dangerous for the faithful. Yet it is quite common for people as they pray, to feel moved with love for God, and for that love to be accompanied by a stirring in the body—for the body is us, not a shell we inhabit. Although Francis would not have talked about it in this sort of language, the lesson he teaches us by his life is to have complete trust in the God who made us; trust that our Creator knows how we function, loves us thus and will lead us to harmony. Everything fell into place and 'worked' for Francis when he placed himself in God's hands. Without God, he knew himself to be greatly at risk, and once shocked his brethren by saying, quite late in his life, 'I may yet have a wife and children.' He learnt that most of us sin more by not loving enough and by being too afraid of the power of love which is in us, rather than by loving too much or inappropriately. Many so-called sins in the area of loving, are really sins of selfishness, not sins of loving. We tend to seek satisfaction, not self-giving.

Although so obsessed with it, our society also has a deep, atavistic fear of the body. Religion has sometimes dealt with this by rejecting either the body, or society, or both. Yet there is a point of balance, where religion can leap free from society's compulsions while still sharing its concerns. Religion should be continually leading people to redemption and transcendence, using the energy of their innate longing for a union of the human and the divine. This is the original model of love as it crosses the boundaries from within to without the Godhead, and we see it embodied in Christ. The prophetic power of religion draws it into a ceaseless interaction with society, always pointing out where God is already present, but hidden, within it. This is *the* prophetic task; like John the Baptist, to point to the hidden Christ and say: There he is! The undeniable power of love in our society is itself just such a presence of God, a hidden incarnation awaiting theophany, the revealing of God.

In our journey to God, every aspect of human living will be brought into play. If we take the incarnation of Christ seriously—and who would wish this more than Francis?—then we cannot regard the physical as second-rate or dubious. One clear message from the stigmata of Francis is that God takes our flesh as seriously as that of Christ. Obviously it would be foolish to ignore the fact that all is not right within us, and that disorder is more native to us than order, or that the prime channel for expressing this is through a powerful sexuality which easily takes the law into its own hands. Yet we are redeemed, an Easter people, and we can trust our redemption. Our personal task, through the continuing process of conversion, sorrow and love, is to make that redemption our own, marked with the marks of Christ. The wounds of Christ on the hands of Francis were visible signs, in one, of the inner truth of us all.

All Francis' spirituality centred around Christ. He imitated him and tried to live as Christ lived, vulnerable and redemptive. We can see a shift in Francis as he developed, from head to heart, from understanding and acceptance to commitment and surrender. We see the same shift in his questions, from: What do you want me to do? to: What more could I do? as his readiness to obey developed into a tested love which could hardly contain its desire to give everything. When we look back, we will see the same shift in ourselves, the same grace at work. By the time of the stigmata, it seems as if Francis was no longer divided within himself in any way, so that when he and God spoke together, his response sprang from the centre of his being, a complete expression of himself. For him, as for us, the work of years had opened spaces for the infinite within his finite self. From the day when he had read Matthew chapter 5 and cried out that this was how he wanted to live, he had walked steadily along a way on which the calligraphy of every jot and tittle of the Law worked to achieve its purpose.

9

Redeemed People

It is a curious characteristic of the Franciscan story that they seem so joyful to us today, as if Francis, Clare and all the early brothers and sisters moved in an atmosphere of springtime. Yet, when we read the contemporary stories about those early days, we find that they are often tales of struggle and misunderstanding. Both Francis and Clare experienced a lot of pain, partly self-inflicted, partly arising from the demands of their own inner growth and development, and partly due to various conflicts within and around the Order. For Francis, there had been endless arguments among the friars about the way their life was meant to be, about whether Francis' ideal was possible or even desirable. After his death there had been trouble with the Minister General, Brother Elias, and apparently irresolvable internal conflicts and rows about poverty. Clare was right at the centre of these conflicts, in the sense that she was one of the most uncompromising witnesses to Francis' vision, although she did not have these internal arguments to contend with at San Damiano. Perhaps her presence was a guarantee against it. What she did have, was a conflict with the Papacy extending over many years, again about the principle of poverty. The Popes wanted her to accept property and security, and to have a fixed, assured income. She had no intentions of doing this. She saw that what Christ had done here on earth was to live at risk and with insecurity, and this was what she would do. As before with Francis, no Pope quite liked to say that it was impossible to live the Gospel literally or to imitate Christ exactly, but neither did they like a group of women with no visible means of support, particularly at a time when many women's religious houses were in grave financial trouble and the Papacy was having to bail them out.

This was the background against which Francis and Clare sought to live as Christ lived, sought to gaze on him continually, daily to become more like him, and so more and more to love God and people and all creation. Their ardour, their joy and their poetry were forged in fires of argument and struggle, amid conflicts of obedience and loyalty. These were not just obstacles to be overcome, but the real material of their lives, the stony soil out of which grew their peace, faith, hope, love and all the other fruits of the Spirit. We are sometimes surprised to find that even people as dedicated to having nothing but God as they were, still had material problems. They still had to struggle with intransigent resources and intransigent people. Their struggle was about how to put the kingdom first, how to leave God free to build, to create out of nothing, but all the same, for them as for us, it was the struggle itself and their handling of it, which moved them to sanctity. We are all honed and polished by the actual process of dealing with intractable things, and particularly by the struggle to retain our peace and sense of humour in this process.

In general the Popes were very ambivalent about the Assisi venture. This created difficulties for Clare, who wanted the Church's blessing on her community, and wanted even more to have that protection from coercion which only the Papacy could bestow, but who was not prepared to compromise on her ideals in the slightest degree. The Papacy was reluctant. There are one or two letters from Pope Gregory IX to Clare, after his visits to her at San Damiano, in which he speaks to her as to a great saint, with love and veneration and admiration. Yet the hard fact is that when he finally and reluctantly ratified the Privilege of Poverty, that unique guarantee, earlier granted her by Innocent III, that no one could force her to have possessions, he drew its teeth in many respects. He confirmed her wish to live in poverty, conceding that 'no one can compel you to receive possessions', but he removed most of the sanctions which were, at that time, essential if the document was to carry much weight. Although he professed such veneration for Francis and Clare, and although he was thought, by Francis at least, to have such sympathy with their ideals, over the next few years he continually offered various Poor Clare houses around Europe relaxations of this commitment to poverty. At times he went so far as to impose these relaxations. Yet in spite of all this, the perspective of history is a true perspective. Against this turbulent background, joy was the colour of the air about them. They knew everything to be

the work of God's creative love, their whole lives were infused
with the glory of this basic insight.

At every turn, their response was spontaneous and quick.
When Francis heard the Gospel of Matthew read and realised
that that was how he wanted to live, he instantly began to put
it into practice, took off his shoes, kept only one tunic and tied
an old rope around his waist. In the same way, Clare saw that
no life can have two masters and acted dramatically on this
insight. Once each had acted on their decision, they began to
discover for themselves the truth of Paul's words that all
things work together for good for those who love God.

By their words and lives, they show us that their simple
secret is to look at God. The rest follows; the mystery is that
by looking at God, we allow God to look at us and the dialogue of this gaze restores us to the joy of our original face;
quite literally, it recreates us. This is exactly what Clare spent
her life telling her sisters to do: gaze on Christ, look at him,
contemplate him if you want to imitate him. As we live with
her advice, it becomes clearer to us that she meant much more
than the externals, much more than behaviour or values. She
certainly did mean those, but first of all she meant learning to
imitate Christ in his relationship with the Godhead.

> Place your mind in the mirror of eternity!
> Place your soul in the splendour of glory!
> Place your heart in the image of the divine substance!
> Through contemplation be completely transformed into the
> image of the Godhead itself.[1]

Give your mind to this reflection of God, she is advising us,
and let your soul be flooded with the splendour of glory. Give
your heart to Christ who is the icon of the divine for us. If you
do this, your whole self, all your being, will gradually be
transformed into another image, another icon, of what God is,
so that all who see you will see God. This is what we mean by
learning to pray. We, people who pray, are always being
invited into the beyond of God. God is like a hall of mirrors, lit
by an infinity of lights, where even our darkness can become
light itself. God is a sea of radiance, where our little boat skims
in an infinite response. God is the final Beloved one, who, in
the end, we all grow to resemble; the Partner in a union which
is not transient but totally, and reassuringly, transforming.

No matter how they are translated or paraphrased, the

intensity of Clare's words is incandescent. Francis was no less intense, but differently so. He would often speak to God as Father, or address each person within the Trinity under a separate title, but Clare preferred more general, and less analytical, phrases like the Most High, the eternal King or simply God. In relation to God, she often spoke of herself and the others as daughters, though they were always sisters in relation to herself. Yet the images of God which resonated for her, were those which touched on God's infinity and glory, on light, brilliance, splendour; all contrasted with our nothingness and poverty. Both Francis and Clare saw that because our nothingness is so great, it is our greatest resource, the most 'God-sized' capacity in all our being. For this reason alone, they would have kept faith with the Lady Poverty.

The more Clare pondered on Christ's unique relationship with the Father, the more she understood the call that we hould be co-workers with Christ. 'To use the very words of the Apostle himself, I think of you as a co-worker of God, one who sustains the members of his body who are failing',[2] she writes to Agnes. This is our task: to 'sustain the members of his body who are failing', and this is what is meant by being a co-worker with Christ. At the same time, because Christ will inevitably lead us further and further into the beyond of God, we may not find resting places even in service, but must journey onwards into deeper mystery and greater clarity. The life of God is accretive, it grows by building on stones already laid, not by clean sweeps and starting again. So it is important that we do not lose heart, but continue doing what we have committed ourselves to do. As early as 1235 she wrote to Agnes saying:

> Hold fast to what you now hold,
> never cease doing what you are doing now,
> but run swiftly, light-footed, unshackled,
> collecting no dust even on your feet,
> so that you go unfalteringly along the road to blessedness
> with certainty, with joy and with speed;
> believe nothing, agree to nothing
> which would lead you to take back what you have given
> or which would place you on a path where you would
>   stumble.[3]

This is reminiscent of a dream Clare had, in which she

climbed towards Francis up a steep stairway, but the nearer she got to him, the more swiftly she travelled, until in the end she was running along as lightly as if she had been on level ground. We all teach each other, she realised, even while we all learn directly from Christ; she taught the sisters, and us, but she herself learnt from Francis, and Francis learnt from Christ. As we become swifter, more light-footed, less shackled, the lessons become easier, the steep pathway less and less of an obstacle.

When we move out of the starters' class and begin the lessons of prayer proper, lessons which will lead us into a new life, the way will certainly feel at times like hard graft, a long slog up a steep stairway. Here Clare's injunction never to cease doing what you are doing now, is excellent advice, especially in view of the way we so easily give up on spiritual things. It was surprising to Clare that the stairway became easier as it grew steeper. So the gifts of prayer will come, slanting in when we least expect it and, often, when we have 'no time' to stay with it. Time is a mysterious component in prayer. It is essential to give prayer time: to give time to it and give it time to develop. It is also true that our prayer has little commerce with time, suddenly taking off at inopportune moments, deserting us when we have settled to give it an hour or so.

For most of our lives, our prayer is best based safely on God's fidelity rather than on anything of ours. While we might envy the great love for God which was Francis and Clare's outstanding gift, we are not always prepared to do what they did in order to learn this love, or to receive this gift. Like many amateurs, we do not really believe the high price of expertise. We insist that there must be a preceding gift, and up to a point this is quite true, but in this case, the gifts are offered to us all, given through looking at Christ with a mind to learn. Francis and Clare believed exactly what God said; we tend to half-believe, to explain, qualify and water down, and in the process we erode the power of the word. When they began, Francis and Clare had no more than we have. Everything they did have was God's gift, offered equally to us. The same power and the same redemption are at work in us as in them.

What, in human terms, did all this do for them? What did it make of them? Can we look at them and think: that is a redeemed person and that is how I want to be? Celano offers

us a most attractive—and in some respects quite surprising—
pen portrait of Francis as a redeemed man, when he says:

> He was charming in his manners, serene by nature, affable
> in his conversation, most opportune in his exhortations,
> most faithful in what was entrusted to him, cautious in
> counsel, effective in business, gracious in all things. He was
> quick to pardon, slow to become angry, ready of wit, ten-
> acious of memory, subtle in discussion, circumspect in
> choosing, and in all things simple.[4]

The most striking aspect of this description is the humanity
of Francis; grace had formed him into himself, all his human
gifts had been brought to God and most delightfully sancti-
fied. To the end of his life he was witty, quick, talkative and
charming just as he always had been; effective in business we
might not have expected, yet he was his father's son and
Pietro had been a most effective up-and-coming businessman.
Celano says a lot more than this, speaking of Francis' elo-
quence, cheerfulness and kindness, and ends up saying that
among holy people, Francis was as one of them, but sinners
too felt that he was one of them. He was at home with everyone, all things to all that he might gain all.

Francis is an outstanding demonstration of something
which we tend to doubt, namely that God loves the person we
already are and has no desire to turn us into stereotyped saints
to adorn his heavenly niches. The saints God likes and seeks
are robust human beings in all our original quirkiness. To
become holy is really to become our dearest selves, for
redemption means to buy back what has been sold into
slavery, to free what is mortgaged. It is often our most endear-
ing aspects which have led us into the most trouble, been our
most wilful or sinful areas. It is quite possible that the reason
why fewer people attain to holiness than are invited to it
(in other words, most of us) is because somewhere we have
persuaded ourselves that holiness is not highly desirable, that
it involves ceasing to be ourselves in some quite essential way,
such as losing our sense of humour or becoming pious. Let us
look at Francis, even Francis with the wounds of Christ in his
body, and take comfort.

We can also be encouraged by Clare's admission that she
knew she had been called so as to give a mirror and example
to people, so that they could see what life they had been

called to live. They could see that she was kind and prayerful, compassionate and gentle, tender to the sick. These were the things she considered essential for our journey into God, not necessarily living in celibacy or being a nun. Indicative of this is the delightful story about the noble who had sent his wife back to her father's house in disgrace about twenty years before, and had now been told by Clare that he should be reconciled with her. This was really bad news to him and he jibbed at it, but Clare smiled gently and sent him home. There he began to be swept by such longing and desire for his wife that he quite changed his mind, he yearned for her to come back to him. Presently, as Clare had prophesied, they had the son who was such a delight to their old age. This does not sound in the least as if Clare secretly thought everyone should be celibate, but rather suggests a tough Latin realism about human beings and the way we usually do exactly what we want to do. The secret is to want the right things.

Francis and Clare knew that we are all invited to share the glory of God. No matter what our role and condition of life, we learn from Christ how to accept this invitation. Christ is the universal exemplar, he is God's advice come alive, God's word in our language. It is impossible to overstress the extent to which they taught us to learn from Christ. This certainly does not mean that they down-played the place of God, the divine being, in our lives. It is quite clear that they both had an intense awareness of the inner, Trinitarian life of God dwelling within them. Francis seems to have been more aware of the diversity of persons within God, and Clare more aware of the oneness of the Godhead. Once again, they are complementary in their perspectives, rather than contradictory. In this sense, it is unnecessary to define too precisely which person within the Trinity Clare has in mind when she tells us that God is

> of such a beauty that the blessed hosts of heaven never
> weary of admiring,
> of such love that we are stirred.[5]

She is telling us what she has learnt herself, basing her certitude on her own experience, and this is what she tries to share with us. She knew it was more important to respond than to understand; she had learnt that everything makes good sense although it may not always appear so. She knew that her part, like ours, was to be open, to receive and to respond to God, to reflect and reflect upon God. In the process of learning such availability she found that

> By such contemplation we are renewed,
> by such kindliness, flooded,
> by such gentleness, filled,
> gently enlightened by such a memory.[6]

As a result, she is able and content to leave her limited under-standing behind.

All their lives Francis and Clare worshipped beauty at its source, and this enabled them to recognise its reflections everywhere they looked. Even in their own lives, always notoriously difficult to judge, they knew the work of God when they saw it. 'The one who created you has made you holy,' Clare said encouragingly to herself as she lay dying, 'The one who created you has filled you with the Holy Spirit and guarded you as a mother guards her child, he has loved you with a tender love.'[7]

Life was a journey of integration which began with their relationships with God, and moved out to embrace other people and the whole created world, leaving themselves rightly alienated in the process. It was the travelling itself which restored order. Because of their journey, humanity's relationship with creation was left quite different from the way it had been before them. They have left us their legacy, the possibility of universal friendliness, needed more badly today then ever before. They did not see this as a last-minute salvag-ing of resources, which is where *we* are dangerously close to being, but as a gift, as the delighted perception of a unity which had always existed in God's designs, as the rediscovery of friends.

We have seen that it was his call to be a brother which taught Francis this new way of relating, and how, as a result, the spiritual world became as much his natural habitat as this world, or more accurately, they were revealed in his one life as one universe. The same is true of Clare, though as always we have fewer stories and fewer quotes. Neither Francis nor Clare ever lost the awareness that the friendship of creation was a gift; when the wolf did not bite and the fire did not burn or the rabbit did not run away, when the cat went and fetched her sewing for her, then this was a compliment and an honour.

Their constant experience was that growth in holiness meant widening circles of communication, a continuing breakdown of barriers, a reaching out and out beyond the divisions which damage and destroy us all. We see another example of this in the remarkable story of Clare's death.

When Clare lay dying, she received a number of visitors, come to pay their respects and say farewell, but there was one group who came not as visitors but as members of the family, brothers and friends of long standing. We find a whole group of Francis' first brothers gathered around her, including Juniper, Angelo, Leo and Rufino, men who embodied the history of the Order. Now they had come together at the end of the legend just as they had been part of its beginning. Angelo, Leo and Clare were among the ones who had most loved and best understood Francis, they were the ones he had relied on, the ones who had first and most thoroughly committed themselves to his vision of total imitation of Christ, the poor man. Rufino her cousin was also one of this group; it was he who had first spoken to her about Francis all those years ago. Brother Juniper was there too, that 'excellent jester of the Lord',[8] who always had new things to tell her about God, freshly learnt in his prayer. This was the same Juniper who had done such bizarre things in his youth, cutting off a pig's foot to feed a sick brother, cooking enough food for a month all at once, so that they would have more time to pray, of whom Francis had said that he wished he had a forest of such Junipers. Now, an old man, we find him still original, still jesting, still so burning with love that when he opened his mouth, words shot like sparks out of the furnace of his heart, says Celano.[9]

By any standard, this was an extraordinary deathbed, for in the evening a crowd of heavenly ladies, dressed in white with golden garlands on their heads, came through the door, led by one even more splendid, who bent over Clare and embraced her. They brought a covering of 'most remarkable beauty' with them, which they all helped to spread over the bed. Sister Benvenuta said at the Canonisation Process that she had actually seen them all come in, that several other sisters had been there, though some of them had been asleep, and she did not know whether they had seen what she had or not. Asked by a cynical cleric if she had been dreaming herself, she replied firmly that she had been awake and well. So around Clare's deathbed were a number of friars, Mary the Mother of the Lord ('one more splendid than the rest'), a vast crowd of heavenly virgins, and the sisters, and they all found a place in the tiny dormitory at San Damiano. Is it any wonder that we, today, find the whole thing like a child's tale?

Yet what was happening, beneath the unusual events and the strangeness of the almost unbelievable account? Clare and Francis were 'heralds of the great King' as Francis had told the robbers all those years ago, and now other Heralds were coming to tell of the approach of that very same King. Clare saw that the Father's call to them had been to keep the memory of Christ's self-emptying green in the Church. To this end, she had understood and preserved Francis' vision of freedom, his 'marriage' to the Lady Poverty. She knew that they themselves were living signs and symbols, mirrors, reminders of the love of the Lord, who kept back nothing of himself for himself, but gave everything to us. This self-giving was the way she expressed her call to be mendicant; the friars travelled around the world as heralds of the great King, but the sisters travelled inwardly, no less far. The ladies dressed in white who came to that deathbed came as heralds from a distant country, to one who was so free that nothing now hindered her from journeying across the borders.

Does this say anything to us, whose lives are probably less marvellously attended, we, who might think it fine for saints but irrelevant, if not apocryphal, anyway? How does it challenge us, who prefer to think our lives too ordinary for God to be revealed through them? This pseudo-humility of ours can be our strongest defence against God, for time and again we have seen that God loves human beings and rashly entrusts himself to us. The old rabbis used to say that we must build a fence around Torah and protect it, that God needs this from us, and the many prescriptions of the law were all part of this fence, this act of protecting God from the rashness of love. God takes great risks in trusting us, Christ became human in great risk and insecurity, and he carried that through to his death on the cross rather than compromise himself as a sign of love. Clare's life of following Christ was also a steady journey towards greater love, she too lived as a traveller and wanted there to be nothing in the way she lived with which love could reproach her. Her inner freedom, like Christ's self-emptying, was basically an attitude to the future, an openness to the infinite. With this perspective, nothing is too ordinary to reveal God. A crowd of white-robed damsels may not come to our deathbed but they were no more than signs of the God who is always present, who sometimes chooses the unusual instead of the usual, as a means of being Immanuel, God-with-us.

Of all the people present in that little room, only the women and men who were still locked in time could transform time and space. For all their radiance, the white-robed ladies could not transform the material from within, though—as they suggested by the cover they spread over Clare—they could adorn it from without. We are all invited to glory and that glory is not entirely in the future since only those who are still immersed in the material, physical world can sweep that world with them on their journey to God. Only those whose own material being has become infused with the spirituality of love, can lift creation to the fulfilment of its destiny as an unspotted mirror of the working of God.[10] Creation's own mysterious quest needs the service of our love as a kind of priesthood, for without humanity as an integral part (rather than as a dominant part) creation is an incomplete circle.

10

A New Creation

St Paul tells us that in Christ there is neither Jew nor gentile, slave nor free, male nor female, but that we are all God's work of art.[1] This bears out something which we have already considered, that holiness breaks down even the most fundamental of barriers, and it also explains why this should be so and where lie the roots of the tree which bears these healing leaves of reconciliation. In his lifetime, Francis had crossed many barriers, within himself, between himself and others, and between others. Stories abound of his interactions with animals and birds, but he also crossed some barriers between Christianity and Islam, even while the Crusades were still being fought. This was at a time when dialogue had never been thought of and the two religions seemed to be on either side of great and impassable divide. Towards the end of his life, Francis was to cross some ultimate and unnameable barrier between himself and God, returning to ordinary life with the wounds of Christ imprinted on his flesh, a living reminder of the presence of God in the flesh of our lives. His own roots were so deep in the humus of Christ's humanity that he himself became this tree of unfailing healing powers, an incarnation of the city of the future where God is.[2]

Through her contemplative prayer, always a unitive activity in its own right, Clare too crossed barriers, not the same ones as Francis, but complementary ones. Her world of operation was within. The physical confines of her life operated on her spirit like a watchglass on the sun, focusing and concentrating its rays until they had the power to ignite a world. By her presence, and by a kind of awe which surrounded her, she was to demonstrate her authority over the hostile, invading forces of Saracens and mercenaries during two separate attacks on Assisi, saving the town as well as the community. As she matured she too became well known for her healing powers, particularly of healing children and the insane, and—like Francis in this—by her power to reconcile those at odds with each other.

There is one story told about Francis and Clare which beautifully illustrates their development, from weakness of one sort or another to a transcendent union with each other in God, which literally enlightened the world. It is said to be apocryphal by some scholars, but all agree that it is true in some essential way, whether it really happened or not. It gives us a glimpse of life to be in the new heaven and the new earth, the quality of relationships which will characterise the new creation, and the subtle interaction of God and humanity which will be the embroidery of the Kingdom.

When Clare and the first group of sisters began to live in community, they had no superior, abbess, prioress or reverend mother. The community operated by consensus, springing out of the Franciscan conviction that the Spirit speaks to the group rather than to individuals, simply because we are not isolated but, as we live in Christ, parts of a whole. The sisters lived very well like this for about three years, but because of the requirements of Church law at that time, they were under pressure to change and establish a more conventional authority structure. Clare was much opposed to this, but she eventually yielded to the persuasions of the Bishops and Francis and reluctantly accepted the office of Abbess.

When she looked around her at other monasteries of the time, she could see that there was a natural progression by which property and riches gradually collected around a religious house, and the abbess, gradually or quickly, became a great feudal lady. She much feared the same happening at San Damiano and wanted to develop a way of exercising authority which was essentially one of service, expressing her commitment to self-dispossession and poverty. She did not want the power of the job to become her own possession in any way. She also had to sort out how to do this within the setting of community involvement and responsibility, so that decisions continued to be made by all the sisters rather than from the top. Together, she and the sisters had to develop new forms of obedience in a consultative context. This all has a remarkably modern ring. Her solutions to these problems are enshrined in the Rule which she wrote at the end of her life and which her sisters today still try to put into practice. In the course of evolving this new style of government and of finding her own level in this unsought position, Clare often felt the need to talk things through with Francis. She also saw him as her Father in God, the one who had mediated God's call to her in the beginning, and, in addition to that, she simply loved him, was nourished by his presence and depleted by too long an absence. That was her side of it.

From his side, Francis did not go to San Damiano very often, partly in order not to give grounds for gossip, partly because he was away a lot and partly because he obviously found women attractive and at that time was afraid to give himself an inch in case he took a mile. Much more than Clare, Francis dealt with himself by working against his weaknesses; she preferred to proceed by transcending them. These are quite simply two different ways of operating, equally valid and equally effective, neither is better than the other; often the option for one or the other is made by temperament as much as by circumstances. So he went rarely but as often as he felt he could, and encouraged her with his advice, but Clare longed to spend more time with him which was not just 'business', perhaps to have a meal with him and to talk together. She asked several times but he always refused. As on other occasions, the brethren saw Clare's needs more clearly than Francis did, and spoke to him about it. It seemed to them, they said, that his behaviour was a little lacking in love, that Clare had been the first plant in his new garden and deserved more care. It was unjust to deny her 'such a little thing as eating with you, especially considering that she gave up the riches and pomp of the world as a result of your preaching', they said firmly, adding that even if she had asked for more than this, he should still grant it to her.

Because Francis too believed that the Spirit spoke through the community, he listened to what the brothers said and, having consented, did so wholeheartedly, agreeing to do whatever they thought right. He suggested that they invite Clare to a meal at St Mary of the Angels. It would be nice for her, he decided, to see the little chapel where she had made her vows, especially since 'she has been cloistered at San Damiano for a long time'. They would have a meal together in the woods and after that he and the brothers would make a return visit to her at San Damiano.

The day came, Clare and her companon were escorted by a

group of brothers to the Portiuncola, the 'Little Portion', and went into the chapel to greet Our Lady, whose house it was. The account then says, rather delightfully, that the brothers showed her round the place until it was mealtime, showing her the little huts where they lived and saying 'This is where . . .' while Francis prepared bread and water on the table of the bare ground, as he usually did. Finally, he and Clare sat down together, one of his companions accompanied Clare's companion and the others sat around too. Before they ate, Francis started to speak about God. Clare always had a great eagerness to hear the Word of God preached, in a way which suggests a ready, questing mind at a time when there was very little intellectual nourishment around for women. Also she had heard Francis preach when she was quite a young child and had never forgotten it. So he began to tell her again about the wonder of God. Now, however, she was grown up and a person of considerable stature in her own right, and merely by her presence she contributed something to the meeting and the dialogue, so that the small glade in the wood became filled with the grace of God. Francis and Clare and all their companions were gradually caught up into heaven, sitting there with their hands and hearts lifted up. It seemed to the people round about that the little wood was on fire and they rushed to the rescue, only to find this rapt group lost in God and 'invested with power from on high'. The people quietly withdrew, realising that what they had seen had been the fire of love. After a long time, everyone came down to earth again, so refreshed and nourished that they forgot about the bread and water waiting humbly on the earth, and accompanied by her sister and the brothers, Clare returned to San Damiano.[3]

This story neatly encapsulates the journey they each made (and the journey each of us is invited to make) out of their own lives and into a world-illuming union with God. It is their life-stories in miniature and it shows us that whatever they themselves had to struggle with, they were a single flame in their love of God, and all Assisi knew it. Through their union in God they helped bring to birth the new creation, for the new heaven and the new earth were already happening in their lives, everything was being revealed in its original face. This new heaven and new earth are characterised by harmony and joy, by time and space fully redeemed, the material

flooded by the spiritual, the everyday lit up by love. There will
be no tears because tears are our response to what has gone
wrong, and all that will be redeemed. All our relationships
will be freed from the incompatibilities which now scar them,
and they will be revealed in their essential generosity and
goodness. The new earth will contain all that is good and
blessed of this earth; all things that are lovely and dear and
funny will find a place there; like Francis and Clare, we
already bring it to pass when we nurture things into the fullness of life. By any reckoning these two were a remarkable
pair of people, but only by following their strange call to lose it
all, could they fulfil their potential and find the enduring glory
of the world in the perfection of the Gospel.

To the cynic of the twentieth century, this sounds like
cuckoo-land and it certainly raises serious questions about sin
and suffering and their place in the ideal world of the future.
Sin and suffering must have a place, because although the new
creation is indeed new, it is also the fruit of the individual
history of each one of us as well as of our collective history.
The new creation grows out of the old and, like it or not, sin is
woven inextricably into the fabric of our lives. Redemption
can never be a simple restoration but a movement forward
into something new. One of the great divides in human
thought is between those who consider our nature to be irre-
trievably ruined and those who never lose their conviction
that human nature is essentially good—which would be
Francis and Clare's position. Either way, holiness can now no
longer mean the absence of sin but the presence of redemption.

In one of his Admonitions, Francis shows how goodness
drives out evil, virtue drives out vice and he lists them in pairs:

Where there is charity and wisdom—there is neither fear
   nor ignorance.
Where there is patience and humility—there is neither
   anger nor disturbance.
Where there is inner peace and meditation—there is neither
   anxiety nor dissipation.
Where there is mercy and discernment—there is neither
   excess nor hardness of heart.

and so on.[4] He does not suggest, on the Augustinian model,
that sin is the absence of these good things, but only that when

the good is there, the bad is not there. It is an application of Christ's counsel to us that we should repay evil with good because the two are mutually exclusive and evil cannot exist where good is. If we are merciful, we are not hard. We tend to operate as if the good will spontaneously happen when the bad has gone, so that when we are no longer angry, we will naturally be patient, but in fact it is the other way round, when we commit ourselves to patience, anger departs. Our problem is not really the philosophical one, but simply that when we are angry we do not want to be patient, when we are hard towards someone, mercy is the last thing we want to feel for them. Yet as always with God, the way through is through, not round. There are no easy, magic answers, but redemption enters our hearts through our own sinfulness when we grapple with the evil in ourselves, that enemy within which colludes with external, objective evil. Redemption happens when we repay evil with good and choose the joy of salvation instead of the gloom of our sinfulness. All this is the building of the Kingdom, the new creation.

Does the same hold true with what might be called great evil, for instance some of the terrible things which have happened in our own century, the genocides, the abuses, the destruction? In the light of those, to be happy seems insulting and joy impossible. Yet is it not true that if these events overwhelm us permanently, then they are indeed running the world? Francis and Clare consistently taught that joy is a sharing in God's life, not what we feel when nothing is going wrong. It is the fruit of previous choices made freely, albeit heroically. It does not require us to deny the reality of sin or pain, but only to deny that they are the greatest thing around. Joy is less transient than happiness; joy is a commitment to the new heaven and the new earth. It is what Clare meant by:

> [this] wonderful vision will make all the citizens of the heavenly Jerusalem blessed.[5]

Their vision of the world was unique in many respects, it seems. In spite of the focus on animals and birds, it was not a nature mysticism like Richard Jeffries' or even Thomas Traherne's, nor was it the cheerful spirit of inquiry which we find, for instance, among the Cambridge Platonists or Sir Thomas Browne who said briskly that the world was made to be inhabited by beasts and contemplated by man. It was certainly not a perspective which saw the world as a universal churchyard, like John Donne. The simplest explanation of their vision is Celano's, that they had recovered original innocence. Celano did not say that explicitly of Clare, but he did say that from quite early on, the friars regarded her as the queen of peace. Francis and Clare walked on the earth like people who were at home, surrounded by friends. They carried with them the one gift which humanity uniquely gives to the universe: the ability to fill the ordinary with love. This is the perfect work of widsom, the hallmark of reconciled people.

Reconciliation is one of the keynotes of Francis' teaching— to forgive, for God's love surely includes the unforgiveable, to forgive when there are no reasons to do so other than God's love for both parties. What Christ recommends to us is continually practised by God, who turns the other cheek and forgives seventy times seven, who lets love pour out like the sun and makes the rain fall whether we deserve it or not. God's 'values' (so to speak) are moulded of joy and love, elements of the divine being, and even when we are distressed, that joy continues to exist, not greater than all our griefs, but different.

Often what we lack is not so much the willingness to be joyful as the skills to be so. These skills are perfected over time, by love, by prayer, by penance, by wanting to learn them, by steadfast generosity and unselfishness in small things, by maturing self-knowledge and by grace. Through our experiences of grief and pain we learn to walk, as Clare said, without any dust sticking to our feet, suggesting that when we have been into dreadful places and survived, then we move through life differently. Yet we know that there is room in God for our distress and that God's response to our pain is Christ, the Word of God spoken in our own language and, perhaps, even embodying an explanation to us for all the seemingly incomprehensible grief. As we learn this language we begin to glimpse the answers, though often not to the questions we had originally asked.

As always with God, everything is different from what we thought, everything is bound up with everything else much more than we had realised, and everything is destined for the joy of the Lord, to be an instrument of delight:

Let everything you have made
be a song of praise to you . . .

Through Brother Wind and Sister Water,
Through Brother Fire and Mother Earth,
Through Sister Death — be praised, O Lord,
be praised.

When we forget the wisdom of reconciliation, we forget how to play, and all creation groans in travail with us; when we remember this wisdom, we begin to hear the true message of creation:

Let everything you have made
be a song of praise to you,
above all, His Excellency the Sun (our brother);
through him you flood our days with light.
He is so beautiful, so radiant, so splendid,
O Most High, he reminds us of you.

The play of wisdom is God's crowning gift to us and we will often find that play is indefinably present in the atmosphere of holy people. In the same way, some of the early Franciscan stories are very funny. They have all the effervescence of a new world bright with love and tell of men sitting lightly to convention, just as the brothers spun like tops at the crossroads until Francis shouted 'Stop'. This light approach, however, is bought at a great price, and, if it is to last, it cannot be just the froth of a new lifestyle but must be rooted in a far-reaching inner dedication. For Francis, it had to mature from that first froth into a far riper vintage. This echoes a slender but tough strand of thought in Scripture dealing with the ideas of play and delight, a strand which finds its best expression in the last great chapters of Job, where God is describing the wonders of creation and asking some unanswerable questions to which Job stutters in response.

What emerges is that for God, creativity is the overflowing of superabundant life into myriad forms, easy, playful and terrible.

Will you make a pet of Leviathan, like a bird,
    keep him on a lead to amuse your maids?
Is he to be sold by the fishing guild
    and then retailed by the merchants? . . .

You have only to lay a finger on him
   never to forget the struggle or risk it again![6]

For us in our limitations, creativity is painfully driven by
our thrust towards transcendence, our Leviathan is certainly
no pet. God, on the other hand, plays with all the universe,
and in the new world of the Kingdom we, too, shall learn
those games of God. The notion of the universe and God
playing like friends, highlights our sense that we are outsiders
in our own world, that our faces are pressed against a window,
looking in on moments of secret understanding, when God
rejoices in the diversity of all that is made. The magic of
Francis for us is that he found his way to God's side of the
window, holding the cricket on his finger, the rabbit in his
arms, reminding the birds to praise God, cautioning the
worms not to live so dangerously, advising the wolf to give up
eating children.

All these stories about Francis share the delight and joy in
creation which we find running through those chapters of Job
(38–41). They are also echoes from a time (in the past or the
future) when we were not alienated from half our world. By
grace, we have been invited into the fullness of life and begin
to find that the new heaven and the new earth are inextricably
entwined with our present world in the simplest possible way.
The one who gave the ibis wisdom (Job 38:36) will do the
same for us, for true wisdom and laughter are gifts, not acqui-
sitions, generous sharings in the divine lifestyle. The melody
of delight we hear in Job and the one we hear in Francis are
from the same song: Who laid the cornerstone (of the earth)
when all the stars of the morning were singing with joy? (38:7)

The Moon and Stars are clear and dear and fair, sang
Francis and

   Brother Fire, robust and glad and strong,
   None shines as he shines in blackest night,
   How handsome he, how joyous and how bright.

God values what is, simply because it is, not insisting that it
be beautiful or useful. When Job grumbles that he has been
reduced to nothing but a companion of the ostrich (30:29),
stalking with ungainly dignity across arid ground, God says:
Ah, but what about the soft feathers, have you noticed those,
they are beyond comparison (39:13)? Then from the heart of

the tempest God talks with loving amusement about some of his animals, Behemoth for instance (clearly a hippo), eating greenstuff, hiding in the reeds of the swamp, a throat big enough for all the Jordan to run through, no one will catch him and run a peg through his nose (40:15–24), or Leviathan on whom we need only to lay a finger once, never to forget or risk it again! (40:32).

Every creature tells us about God, as Francis well knew. The stirring passages in Job about the mystery of birth, the freedom of the wild donkey, the improvidence of the ostrich, the fierce neighing of the wild horse laughing at fear and eating up the miles, the soaring of the hawk and the eagle, feeding their young on blood and watching for prey from unclimbable peaks, are all echoes of a being whose greatness is to do with the untrammelled play and interplay of a unique nature. God is both ferocity and tenderness, laughter and high seriousness, awe-inspiring and gentle. We will never understand how the pairs fit together, but every day in the created world we meet them all, realities in their own right but also parables. 'Let every creature, in heaven, on earth, in the sea and in the depths, give praise, glory, honour and blessing to God . . .' [7]

As Francis and Clare knew so well, God is greater than all, God is utterly Other,

> without beginning, without end,
> unchangeable, invisible,
> indescribable, ineffable,
> incomprehensible, unfathomable,
> blessed, worthy of praise,
> glorious, exalted on high, sublime,
> most high, gentle, lovable,
> delectable and totally desirable
> above all else forever. Amen. [8]

We are invited into all this, summoned to the familiar and the unknown, to risk and danger, delight and peace, to the Kingdom, to the new creation. Francis and Clare constantly had to remake their theology in the light of their honest experience, and so will we. They had no wish for a tamed God living in a gilded cage of explanations. This throwing open of the mind is the beginning of the Kingdom. It is what Clare meant when she tells us: Through contemplation be transformed into the image of the Godhead itself.[9]

The wisdom of their choice of poverty begins to emerge, because it gave them the space of heart to look around the world and appreciate it, to greet others inhabiting our planet, to explore the mystery of God. By committing themselves to the exacting discipline of not being possessive in any way, they were able to lead creation to holiness, and Francis blamed himself because he had not preached to the birds before, says Celano.[10] Because they were free, they set others free, enabling them to reach God. In the same way, creation today waits for us to lead it out of groaning into a condition where the monsters of the deep are again God's playmates and where human happiness transfigures the face of the earth.

Without doubt, holiness is our greatest ecological contribution. Without it, we shall never balance the needs and rights of our diversified world. Holiness is restoration of order in its most searching and creative form, an unfailing source of respect for others. The reason why Francis is such an appropriate patron for ecological movements is not so much because he preached to the birds and rescued worms from the dangers of the road, but because he approached all that is made with a respect bordering on reverence. Beyond that, he preached reconciliation to us all: Let us love our neighbours as ourselves, he says and adds realistically: and if there is anyone who does not wish to love them as himself, at least let him do no harm to them, but rather good.[11] Put like that, it sounds minimal; put into practice, it would solve many of the problems we anguish over.

Surely it is in this ministering to creation with love, which only we human beings can do, that our 'stewardship' mainly consists? Stewardship does not mean surrogate ownership, nor domination, but it means service, within narrow parameters, leading to a predetermined end. Not everything is for our use or domestication, though we have often made the mistake of thinking it so. Only by high-quality human service will our planet be transfigured by love and enabled to do 'better than its best'; like Francis' cricket, whose readiness to try a new way of living is an example to us all, this spirit of readiness is a fruit of the Kingdom, itself the only thing, Clare says, that we can place any reliance on.[12] There is no reason why we too should not learn to delight in life, learn to play before God as Francis did and Clare did. We need only keep in mind the wonderful words of Gregory of Nyssa that we go from beginning to beginning by beginning without end! The first beginning of all is the wish to start. 'One thing alone is necessary', said Clare to Agnes, 'I bear witness to it, and I encourage you, so that you will always remember your own beginnings.'[13]

Communion, like the Kingdom, is not deferred until we are perfect, just as conversion is never over but goes on (it seems) for ever and contrition is never redundant or unnecessary. God welcomes such love as we are able to give now, responding to it and honouring the fact that we humans only learn to love by loving, that neither thought nor instincts can replace practice for us. As we draw nearer to God, we increasingly share in the divine liking for human beings, which, when we are at the receiving end, is one of the marks of holiness we most appreciate, especially in view of the fact that holy people are often the very ones to whom we confide about our less likeable aspects. As we too grow a little holy, Clare's prayer for us begins to be answered: that we should know 'what it is that the friends of God taste, what is that hidden sweetness, that which God has kept from the beginning, like a secret, for those who love him'.[14]

It was a long journey for Francis from the pit in Assisi to that strange vision on La Verna, but out of the tensions of such a fusion came his great hymn of praise to God, and then his song of praise for all creation. In terms of apostolic activity, he did very little after that, as much as anything for the practical reason that the stigmata made it painful and difficult for him to walk, he was nearly blind and his general health was in ruins. In terms of incarnating the fruits of a lifetime's spiritual quest, he did everything. In the same way it was a long journey for Clare from her solitary flight from her father's house to that reassurance to herself on her deathbed that she could go forth in peace because she had a good escort. In between, shining through all the stories about them both, we see a new way of living which speaks to us clearly about the new heaven and the new earth, when all things will be made new and God will be all in all, God who Clare tells us is

> of such a beauty that the blessed hosts of heaven
>   never weary of admiring,
> of such love that we are stirred.[15]

This love, she tells us, moves us to our depths and by gazing at
it we are so graciously restored and refreshed that, even
though the resultant insights may be plain truths about ourselves, we are able to receive them peacefully as gentle enlightenment.

> By such contemplation we are renewed.
> by such kindliness, flooded,
> by such sweetness, filled,
> gently enlightened by such a memory,
> God is a fragrance to bring the dead to life again,
> a vision of such glory as to bless all those who
> dwell in Jerusalem on high.[16]

It is a hallmark of grace that we rejoice to know the truth.
However dead we feel, there is in God that which always
restores us to life, just as in God there is such glory that even
those already blessed in Jerusalem feel blessed again. Clare's
final touch is to tell us that when we have eaten such food and
drunk at such a banquet, we too share in what God is, not the
glory itself but the splendour of it, not the eternal light itself
but its brilliance.

> She[17] who has shared this holy banquet
> is herself the splendour of eternal glory,
> the brilliance of eternal light,
> and the unspotted mirror.

Having gazed long into the mirror of Christ, in the crib
and on the Cross, we ourselves become what Christ is, the
unspotted mirror of wisdom reflecting the unimaginable glory
of Jerusalem. Even we will taste that hidden sweetness which
God has kept from the beginning, like a secret; we too will be
kissed with the most joyful kiss of God's lips.

The Canticle of Creation
by
Francis of Assisi

Praise and glory, honour and blessing
Be yours, O Lord,
O Most High
O Most Powerful.

Praise and glory, honour and blessing
Be yours, O Most High.
O my Lord, be praised.

Let everything you have made
be a song of praise to you,
above all, His Excellency the Sun (our brother);
through him you flood our days with light.
He is so beautiful, so radiant, so splendid,
O Most High, he reminds us of you.

My Lord, be praised
through our Sister the Moon and through each Star.
You made them so clear and precious and lovely
and set them in the heavens for all to see.

Through Brother Wind and Sister Water,
Through Brother Fire and Mother Earth,
Through Sister Death — be praised, O Lord,
be praised.

The Moon and Stars are clear and dear and fair,
Through them be praised, and through the Clouds and Air
By which you nourish us each changing day;
Through precious Water, pure in every way,
So useful, humble, chaste, receive our song.

Through Brother Fire, robust and glad and strong,
None shines as he shines in blackest night,
How handsome he, how joyous and how bright.
O my Lord, be praised!

Let everything you have made
be a song of praise to you,
above all, our Sister, our Mother, Lady Earth
who feeds and rules and guides us.
Through her you give us fruits and flowers
rich with a million hues.
O my Lord, be praised.

Be praised, my Lord,
through those who forgive for your love,
through those who are weak,
in pain, in struggle,
who endure with peace,
for you will make them Kings and Queens,
O Lord Most High.

Through Death, O Lord, be praised,
through our Sister Death,
our Sister Death of the body.
No one who lives can escape from Sister Death.
How terrible for those who have died already from sin;
How blest for those who are alive in Your most holy will,
no further death can harm them.

Notes

CHAPTER I   THE BEGINNING OF CONVERSION

1   Thomas of Celano was a contemporary of Francis, but it seems that they never actually met, itself an illustration of how quickly the Order grew and expanded. There is no doubt of Celano's admiration for Francis, nor that he gathered much of his material from first-hand witnesses.
2   For an account of this episode, see Celano's *First Life* of St Francis (1 Celano) 10, in *St Francis of Assisi, Omnibus of Sources* (Franciscan Herald Press 1972), hereafter called *Omnibus*.
3   St Augustine, *De Dono Perseverentiae*.
4   cf. 1 Celano 4.
5   Admonition V; from *Francis and Clare, The Complete Works*, trs. Regis J. Armstrong OFM, CAP and Ignatius C. Brady OFM, (The Classics of Western Spirituality, Paulist Press 1982), hereafter called *Armstrong Writings*, p. 29.
6   1 Celano 10.
7   1 Celano 2.
8   *Rule of Clare*, VI.
9   Clare, *Letter 1*, 21.
10 Clare, *Letter 1*, 30.

CHAPTER 2   OUT OF THE PIT

1   1 Celano 10.
2   From the *Areopagitica*.
3   1 Celano 11.
4   1 Celano 16.
5   Celano, *Second Life* of St Francis (2 Celano) 9, in *Omnibus*.
6   cf. 1 Celano 17.
7   ibid.
8   1 Celano 18; cf. 1 Cor. 3:11.
9   *Admonitions* V, *Armstrong Writings*, p. 29.
10 *Testament of Clare* 14.

11 This is a debated question and I base myself on the *Omnibus*, p. 877.
12 *Three Companions* 12, *Omnibus*, p. 901.

CHAPTER 3   A PLACE IN WHICH TO PRAY

1 Isaiah 41:14.
2 *We Were With St Francis*, the Legend of the Three Companions, trs. Salvator Butler OFM (Edizioni Porziuncola 1984), p. 19.
3 Clare, *Letter 3*, 12–13.
4 ibid., 3, 7.
5 ibid., 24, 25.
6 ibid., 8.
7 ibid., 27–28.
8 ibid., 26.
9 Clare, *Letter 4*, 15, 17, 18.
10 ibid., 23.
11 ibid., 24–25.
12 ibid., 20. We need to have in mind that mirrors in those days were usually highly polished, convex, metal surfaces. Along with so much else, the art of silvering glass was on the point of being re-taught to Europe by the Arabs. It is also helpful to know that mirrors sometimes had the face of a renowned beauty—Eleanor of Aquitaine, for example—engraved in the centre of them, about where Clare speaks of seeing Christ crucified.
13 Clare, *Letter 4*, 22–25.
14 ibid., 15, 16.
15 cf. Francis, *Rule of 1223*, X *Armstrong Writings*, p. 144.
16 *We Were with St Francis*, p. 72.
17 *Mirror of Perfection*, 123, *Omnibus*, p. 1263.
18 Cf. *We Were with St Francis*, p. 180.

CHAPTER 4   THE PENANCES WE CHOOSE

1 2 Celano 129.
2 cf. 1 Celano 38.
3 1 Celano 40.
4 2 Celano 22; *Legend of Perugia* 1, *Omnibus*, p. 977.
5 Clare, *Letter 3*, 41.
6 cf. 1 Celano 103.
7 Clare, *Letter 3*, 38–39.
8 *We Were with St Francis*, 126.
9 cf. 1 Celano 39.
10 Clare, *Letter 1*, 20.

11 *Admonition* V, *Omnibus*, p. 80.
12 *We Were with St Francis*, 104.
13 ibid., 73.
14 Clare *Letter 3*, 6.
15 Clare, *Letter 1*, 8.
16 Breviary, December 30, Readings, 2nd Lesson.
17 *Admonition* XIII, *Omnibus*, p. 83.
18 *Admonition* XIX, *Armstrong Writings*, p. 33. Bonaventure, in his *Legenda Maior*, tells us that Francis 'had these words continually in his mouth'.

CHAPTER 5   THE PAIN WE DO NOT SEEK

1 *Legend of Perugia*, 109, *Omnibus*, p. 1084.
2 *Testament of Clare*, 38.
3 1 Celano 113.
4 *Life of Clare*, Preface, *Clare of Assisi, Early Documents* ed. and trs. Regis Armstrong OFM, CAP. (Paulist Press 1988), p. 189; hereafter called *Armstrong Sources*.
5 1 Celano 117. This passage and 1 Celano 116 are both sources for this chapter.
6 *Testament of Clare*, 39.

CHAPTER 6   BROTHERS, SISTERS AND MOTHERS OF THE LORD

1 *Letter to Brother Leo, Armstrong Writings*, p. 47.
2 Clare, *Letter 2*.
3 *First Letter to All the Faithful, Armstrong Writings*, p. 63.
4 *Rule of Clare*, VIII.6.
5 *Salutation of the Blessed Virgin Mary, Armstrong Writings*, p. 149.
6 ibid., p. 150.
7 Clare, *Letter 3*, 24, 25.
8 Francis, *First and Second Letters to All the Faithful, Armstrong Writings*, pp. 63, 70.
9 *Testament of Clare*, 19–23.
10 *First Letter to All the Faithful, Armstrong Writings*, p. 63.
11 Form of Life given by Francis to Clare, *Armstrong Writings*, pp. 44–5.
12 Written for Brother Leo, *Armstrong Writings*, pp. 99–100.
13 Francis, *Rule of 1221*, XXIII, *Armstrong Writings*, pp. 133–4.
14 ibid., I.1; *Rule of 1223*, I.1; *Armstrong Writings*, pp. 109, 137. *Rule of Clare*, I.1.
15 *Second Letter to All the Faithful, Armstrong Writings*, p. 67.
16 Matthew 19:21.
17 *Admonition* II, *Armstrong Writings*, p. 27.

18 *Sacrum Commercium*, an allegory on poverty written very soon after the death of Francis, *Omnibus*, p. 1553.
19 Clare, *Letter 1*, 15–17.
20 Canticle written by Francis for Clare and her sisters, *Armstrong Sources*, p. 250.
21 Francis, *Rule of 1221*, XVII, *Armstrong Writings*, p. 123.
22 *Admonition* XXI, *Armstrong Writings*, p. 34.
23 Clare, *Letter 1*, 21.

CHAPTER 7   BROTHER FRANCIS AND SISTER CLARE

1 *We Who were With Him*, 181.
2 *Salutation of the Virtues, Armstrong Writings* p. 152.
3 2 Celano 166.
4 *We Who were With Him*, 124.
5 ibid., 120; also 2 Celano 166 and 171.
6 Ruth 1:16.
7 *Testament of Clare*, 55; *Rule of Clare*, VI.6.
8 Canonisation Process 14, 9; *Armstrong Sources*, p. 169.
9 *Rule of Clare*, VI.1; *Testament of Clare*, 24.
10 All this passage is taken from *Life of Clare*, 24–26, *Armstrong Sources*, pp. 213 ff.
11 *Letter of Agnes, Armstrong Sources*, p. 105.
12 Canonisation Process 2, 10, *Armstrong Sources*, p. 136.

CHAPTER 8   AN INCARNATION OF THE INCARNATION

1 1 Celano 91–96 is the basis of all this chapter.

CHAPTER 9   REDEEMED PEOPLE

1 Clare, *Letter 3*, 12–13.
2 ibid., 8.
3 Clare, *Letter 2*, 11–14.
4 1 Celano 83.
5 Clare, *Letter 4*, 10–11.
6 ibid., 11–12.
7 *Life of Clare*, 46; Canonisation Process 11, 3, *Armstrong Sources*, pp. 229 and 162.
8 *Life of Clare*, 45, *Armstrong Sources*, p. 228.
9 ibid.
10 Wisdom 7:24 (Authorised Version)

CHAPTER 10   A NEW CREATION

1 Ephesians 2:10.
2 Ezekiel 48:35.
3 The *Little Flowers of St Francis*, ch. 15, is the basis for this story.
4 *Admonition* XXVII, *Armstrong Writings*, p. 35.
5 Clare, *Letter 4*, 13.
6 Job 40: 29–32.
7 Francis, *Second Letter to All the Faithful, Armstrong Writings*, p. 71.
8 Francis, *Rule of 1221*, XXIII; *Armstrong Writings*, p. 134.
9 Clare, *Letter 3*, 13.
10 1 Celano 58.
11 *Second Letter to All the Faithful, Armstrong Writings*, p. 69.
12 Clare, *Letter 3*, 26.
13 Clare, *Letter 2*, 10, 11.
14 Clare, *Letter 3*, 14.
15 Clare, *Letter 4*, 10.
16 ibid., 11–13.
17 ibid., 14. This is a debatable translation, but the Latin definitely gives the feminine pronoun *quae* here. It has been assumed by translators that this is a mistake on Clare's part, that she meant to refer to Christ, yet the text will sustain the interpretation that she is speaking about the one to whom such a vision is given and it would be fully consonant with her thinking to have done so.

For Further Reading

Contemporary Writings

Francis and Clare, The Complete Works, ed. and trs. Regis J. Armstrong OFM, CAP and Ignatius C. Brady OFM, in The Classics of Western Spirituality Library (Paulist Press 1982)

Clare of Assisi, Early Documents, ed. and trs. Regis J. Armstrong OFM, CAP (Paulist Press 1988)

St Francis of Assisi, Omnibus of Sources (Franciscan Herald Press 1972)

We Were with St Francis, trs. Salvator Butler OFM (Edizioni Porziuncola, Assisi 1984)

Modern Writings

David Flood OFM and Thadée Matura OFM, *The Birth of a Movement* (Franciscan Herald Press 1975)

Leonardo Boff, *Saint Francis* (Crossroad 1982)

Carlo Carretto, *I, Francis* (Collins 1980)

Brother Ramon SSF, *A Hidden Fire* (Marshall Pickering 1985)

Marco Bartoli, *Clare of Assisi* (Darton, Longman and Todd forthcoming)